Yes, You Can Have the Recipe

Favorite Recipes from the Husum Riverside Bed & Breakfast

Connie Nice

Angela ~ Enjoy!
From my heart and
kitchen to yours. ♡
Connie Nice

Connie Nice

ISBN:1973886634
ISBN-13:978-1973886631

DEDICATION

This collection of photographs, recipes, and stories are dedicated to my family who provide the inspiration behind my cooking and baking. It is also dedicated to our guests who have visited the Husum Riverside Bed & Breakfast and encouraged me to "take a chance" and produce a cookbook of their favorite breakfast moments.

Connie Nice

CONTENTS

Connie Nice

ACKNOWLEDGMENTS

A wise friend and renowned chef once told me, "There really are no truly original recipes." That being said, most of my cooking and baking has been inspired by a variety of sources, including my travels, my family, the Food Network, and Pinterest. I have endeavored, wherever possible, to credit the original source. I truly feel that recipes, mine included, are designed to be challenged, changed, and adjusted to be fully experienced "to taste." Enjoy!

A shout out to my friend Elizabeth Griffith for her "editing eyes" that helped me clean up all the little messy details.

Special hugs go to my husband (David), who spent hours fighting with revisions to the template to help produce my finished draft. I also could not have finished this cookbook without the support of my son and daughter-in-law (Aaron and Lindsey), my daughter (Rachel), and my grandson ("little" Aaron), as well as my mom (Dee). They have created, tasted, photographed, and walked with me throughout this whole process. That's just what family does.

Connie Nice

FOREWORD

By Chef Kathy Watson

I knew of Connie before I met her. She was the director of our local museum, and friends of mine on the board spoke highly of her. She seemed to be everywhere, promoting the museum and talking up local history.

But, I was far too buried in my restaurant kitchen to pay much attention. I was the chef and owner of Nora's Table, a busy breakfast and dinner farm-to-table restaurant in Hood River, Oregon, on the shores of the spectacular Columbia River Gorge. Days came and went when I barely saw daylight beyond visiting my farmers' fields, or starlight until I was walking out of the restaurant late at night at the end of a long dinner service.

Events I couldn't have imagined at that point in my life brought us together. Connie and her family bought a lovely bed and breakfast with a full commercial kitchen just across the river from me in Husum, Washington. And my husband and I decided it was time to retire. When I heard that the Nice's had bought Husum Riverside Bed and Breakfast, it triggered a memory. I visited the B&B years before and had filed away in my mind what a nice kitchen it had, with a lovely patio and arbor along the White Salmon River. What a great place for intimate dining, I thought.

Now, here I was, eight months after selling Nora's Table, recovering from foot surgery and rolling around on a knee scooter at the Columbia Center for the Arts, and there was Connie too, visiting the gallery.

I said, "You know, Connie, I've been thinking I might like to do some dinners, sort of a supper club, just once a month. I love your place. Would you be interested in partnering with me?"

Her eyes lit up. In fact, they'd been serving dinners, on the weekends, Connie and her son Aaron, daughter Rachel and husband Dave. Aaron, an accomplished home cook, was the chef. But now he was moving to Tacoma to marry Lindsey, the love of his life, and the dinners were ebbing away. We began long conversations about food and service and Connie's love of Germany and European hospitality, and then Connie said, "Why don't you come be our guest for breakfast?"

Not all bed and breakfasts are created equal. Many years ago, my husband, Stu, was traveling across Alaska where lodging is scarce, and most homes—mobile, cabins and otherwise -- claimed to be "bed and breakfast" lodging. Staying in the back bedroom of a thin-walled mobile home, he woke the next morning to the sound of his hosts arguing over who would have to fix him breakfast.

Connie and Husum Riverside Bed and Breakfast are in another universe. One where breakfast is revered, where hand-baked pastries and egg cups and handmade yogurt and fruits, cheeses and cured meats are artfully arranged and presented, where the scent of German semmel rolls wafts into the courtyard before you even reach the door of the kitchen dining room.

Connie and Dave buzz about the kitchen, laying out an extravagant breakfast, explaining each item to guests whose eyes rove over the abundance, clutching a plate, anxious to fill it. Grand kids come and go through the kitchen door, and the mood is light and friendly, if a plate groaning with a scone, a fresh roll, a baked ramekin of eggs, mushrooms and bacon, a bowl of homemade granola and the Nice's own yogurt, and so much more, can be described as light.

This is not a toss-off menu, cobbled together by whatever happens to be in the pantry. At my first breakfast, Connie told me about her long effort to recreate the semmel rolls served at so many tables in Germany. Not just any roll would do. It would need to satisfy her memory, be true to the music. The recipe she developed uses whey from their yogurt, and is dense and chewy without being heavy, a roll that just might have you humming, "Um pa pa, um pa pa," to some far-off German band, strolling a cobble-stoned street in an old country village.

As guests hounded Connie for these genuine, carefully crafted dishes, she let herself imagine what it would be like to share them.

I'm glad she did. Recipes and cookbooks are certainly not a rare thing. Want an apple cake? Simply Google it and 100 recipes will be at your fingertips in mere seconds. But you will know very little about the cook who created each one, whether they generated a new idea, or merely copied and pasted an old trope, a worn-out notion of what makes an apple cake. Connie has instead put hours of time into making these dishes again and again for hungry diners staying in the artfully designed rooms of the B&B. They contain the usual ingredients ... flour, sugar, eggs, here and there a pinch of this or that ... and something else: soul.

And yes, Connie and I and the rest of the very nice Nice family, did indeed start a dinner series, the Husum Riverside B&B Supper Club. I cook, whatever suits my fancy, one weekend a month through the spring and summer, and Connie lends her creativity to designing the tables to fit whatever theme I've chosen. By June, the wisteria has enchanted the arbor, and we've burst out on the brick patio, 30 or 40 diners. Connie and the whole family serve, my helpers and I cook, a local winery comes to pour.

And a few lucky ones spend the night, and wander down from one of the inn's rooms, to breakfast the next morning.

Connie Nice

1 BREAKFAST

My first real memory of breakfast is deeply rooted in BACON.

My grandmother lived in an old depression era farmhouse in Ashland, Oregon. When we visited her overnight, we would get to sleep in the upstairs bedroom with the big, creaky, metal bed. The room was located directly above the kitchen. Grandma always cooked on a wood stove and around seven o'clock each morning she would fire up the stove and call up the stairs, "Breakfast!" Of course, my sister Diane and I would just snuggle deeper into the cozy quilts and pretend to not hear her. But then, she would start cooking the bacon. The smell floated up the stairs, through the door and ignited our morning hunger. Leaping from bed we would quickly pull on our clothes – no one was allowed to eat at Grandma's table in their pajamas – and run down the stairs. We may have tried to ignore Grandma, but you just can't ignore the smell of bacon. My love of breakfast was born.

Fast forward to my first experience of European travel with my mom. I was a Sophomore in high school, and she was my German teacher. That is how I found myself experimenting with the taste of Goulash Soup, Roasted Chicken, Sacher' Torte and Kaiserschmarrn. But my favorite food of all time from our many travels to Germany and Austria has to be the simple traditional morning breakfast.

It starts and ends with the roll. A Semmel roll to be exact, however I have since learned that in other parts of Europe it is referred to simply as Brötchen or, "little bread." It is crunchy and flaky on the outside, soft and chewy on the inside, and perfect with either cream cheese and jelly or sliced meats and cheese. For me, it was always a struggle to decide what flavor option to choose, so I would make it open-faced, both ways to experience this staple roll to its fullest taste value. Add some fresh fruit, a few cucumbers with tomatoes, and a great cup of sweet, hot coffee with cream and you have the perfect start to your day.

With my love of German-Austrian breakfast, it was easy to start making choices of what we would serve to our B&B guests when we opened the Husum Riverside Bed & Breakfast in 2015. First on the list – Semmel! But it proved harder than I anticipated to find a method of creating this unique and distinctive roll every single day. In Germany, the woman of the house gets up in the morning and takes a short walk over the cobblestone streets to the corner bakery and buys however many rolls she might need for the day. I did not have that luxury. Armed with a traditional Semmel recipe, I visited all our local bakeries with no luck. Then one day my husband presented me with a book he had found in the airport on a recent trip. The concept of the book was a basic dough recipe that could be revised and adapted and made in advance for a variety of styles of breads and rolls. And there in the table of contents was the Brötchen I so earnestly desired to create. With this crucial component now in place, we began to test and create what is now known by our guests as our "5-star European Breakfast Buffet." Over the past few years, I've taken my initial thoughts on a traditional European style breakfast buffet and "tweaked" it here and there to best fit our needs and maximize the availability of fresh local ingredients. I've developed ways for many of the recipes to adapt to the needs of guests with special dietary requests or restrictions, and I've loved every minute of it. Now, it's your turn. What's your favorite breakfast memory? What do your family members crave from your table when they are traveling or have moved away to start their own families? What's on your breakfast table?

Semmel / Brötchen
"little bread"

Ingredients:
- 3 egg whites
- Hot tap water
- 1 Tbsp dry active yeast
- 1 Tbsp salt
- 7 cups flour
- Whey (optional)

Dough

Put egg whites in a 4-cup measuring cup. Add hot tap water to reach a total volume of 3 cups. Add 1 Tbsp of dry active yeast and 1 Tbsp of salt. Let rest for 5 minutes.

Then add 7 cups all-purpose flour. Mix in your mixer with a dough hook (or by hand) for 10 minutes. The dough should be fully incorporated and spring back when you touch it. Let raise for 1 hour until doubled in size.

Notes:
- I typically substitute some liquid whey (by-product of making homemade yogurt) for some of the water. I add it to the egg whites to reach the 1 cup measuring line, then finish it off with the hot water. I have read you can substitute whey entirely for your liquid when baking. Whey increases the dough's airiness and fluffy texture which helps it raise. Try it. If you're not making yogurt you can purchase a powdered whey product and reconstitute it with your water.
- I have a collection of big 6-quart clear tubs with tight seal lids that I use to raise the dough in. I just set it on the counter and come back later to put it in the cooler.
- These rolls are what we serve every morning at the

B&B. I keep the dough in the cooler for up to 5 days. Just pull off and form however many rolls you want to serve that morning and follow the directions for raising and baking.

Raising and Baking

Rolls should be 2" apart on your baking sheet prepared with spray, parchment paper, or a silicone mat. When you are ready to finish, raise, and bake your rolls, pull off small peach size pieces of dough, quickly knead and shape into balls. Let rolls raise for 20 minutes in a warm place (or proofing oven). This recipe makes 12 – 15 rolls depending on how large you make them.

After 20 minutes, brush the tops of the rolls with a beaten egg white. Then take your kitchen scissors and cut deep x's in the rolls. Hold the scissors straight up and down and don't be afraid to cut deep.

Place a shallow pan on a lower rack and add water to create steam during baking. Bake in a pre-heated oven at 450°F for 9 - 12 minutes. Every oven is different, so the first time you make these watch them carefully. They are done when golden white/brown and sound hollow when tapped. Remove from the pan to cool and serve with cream cheese and jelly or deli meat and cheeses. These make great sandwich rolls as well.

Recipe inspired by *The New Artisian Bread in Five Minutes a Day* by Jeff Hertzberg, M. D. and Zoe Francois

Greek Yogurt

I have never been a fan of yogurt. I have, over the years, attempted to consistently consume it because I thought it was good for me. It wasn't until we started making our own that I truly fell in love with yogurt. Our wonderful, fluffy, home-made, Greek yogurt has become a guest favorite, especially when served with fresh local berries.

Ingredients:
- 1 – gallon WHOLE milk. You can use a quart or other quantity if you want less finished yogurt. We use one gallon and end up with approximately 2 quarts of finished yogurt.
- 1 – 8 oz carton of Greek yogurt with active cultures

Empty milk into a large pan. Heat on medium heat until it reaches 180° F (should have foamy bubbles around the edge of the pan).

Pour into the ceramic crock insert from a crock pot.

Let it cool at room temperature until it is as close to 115°F as possible! This needs to be exact. Get yourself a good quality thermometer and be sure and keep checking and calibrating it before you use it each time.

Once it cools to the correct temperature, add 1 cup of yogurt starter. This can be left-over yogurt from your last batch or a good quality store bought Greek yogurt. When we don't have any yogurt left, we use either vanilla or honey flavor. Stir / whisk until this is thoroughly combined.

Put the lid on the crock and wrap it in a layer of old towels. You want to create a warm, incubating environment. Now comes the hard part. You need to keep this at 105° – 115°F for 8 – 12 hours. We have a warming oven that temperature, but for the home cook, you will need to use your regular oven. Preheat to 350°F. Once it reaches temperature, shut it off. **Leave the oven light on**. Put your yogurt crock in the oven. **Then leave it alone!** Resist the temptation to look at it or unwrap it or open the oven door. You are creating a warm consistent temperature environment.

After 8 – 12 hours (we like to leave ours overnight), spoon the

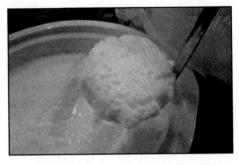

yogurt into a large hole strainer lined with cheese cloth. It should be mostly solid with some liquid base. Put in the refrigerator to sit for another 12 hours. The draining of the whey is the part of the process that changes it from regular yogurt to Greek yogurt. I had a guest recently call it yogurt cheese.

Don't throw away all that whey. There are a ton of ways (lol) to use that funny yellow liquid. Whey protein is considered a complete protein as it contains all 9 essential amino acids. It is low in lactose content and basically flavorless.

1. Soak grains, beans or nuts
2. Make dough for pizza or breads
3. Add it to smoothies
4. Condition your face, hair or body
5. Feed to the chickens
6. Water your plants

The final step to finish the yogurt is to whip it with a hand mixer. Add 2 - 3 Tbsp. honey and 2 Tbsp. vanilla (to taste). Whip to combine. It should be creamy, fluffy, and ready to serve...or just sit and eat it like ice cream, which is our grandkids' favorite way to enjoy it.

Maple Cinnamon Granola with Coconut

We started making our own granola as a cost saving effort and then found we loved it!

Ingredients
- 4 cups old fashioned oats (not instant)
- 2 tsp cinnamon
- ⅓ cup light brown sugar
- ½ cup shredded coconut
- ½ cup sunflower kernels
- ½ cup pure maple syrup (be sure it's pure – not just flavored)
- ⅓ cup vegetable oil
- 1 ½ tsp vanilla extract

Directions
Preheat oven to 325°F. Prepare a rimmed baking sheet with parchment paper or a silicone baking mat.

In a large bowl, combine all ingredients. Stir well to be sure everything is coated. Transfer to your baking sheet. Spread out into an even layer, pressing down to compress the mixture.

Bake for 35 – 40 minutes. You can tell when it's almost done – it will start to smell really good. I test mine by pressing gently with my finger. If it is still somewhat soft, but brown along the edges, it's done. You don't want to over-bake, or it will be really dry. Remove from the oven and cool. Once cool, break the granola into pieces and store in an airtight container for up to 2 weeks.

This is gluten-free (providing the oats you purchased say gluten-free on the label).

Inspired by Baked by Rachel / Pinterest

*Traveling in Germany with my husband, David, my mother,
Dee, and my son, Aaron. We are eating Zwiebelkuchen.*

*Octoberfest at the B&B
with my daughter, Rachel.*

*Mom and I in
Oberammergau, Austria*

Savory Parmesan Waffle

A non-traditional twist on a classic family favorite. This recipe makes 8 small waffles.

Mix Together:
- 1 ¼ cups all-purpose flour
- 1 Tbsp sugar
- 2 tsp baking powder
- ½ tsp salt
- ½ tsp pepper

Note: You can make this in advance and save it in a jar, ready for your final morning preparation.

Combine:
- ¾ cup milk (I prefer whole – but 2% would work)
- ¼ cup unsalted butter – melted
- 2 eggs

Add:
- 1 cup frozen shredded hash browns
- ½ cup shredded parmesan cheese

Finish:
Combine your dry ingredients and wet ingredients, hash browns and cheese, and mix well. Spoon a ladleful into your pre-heated waffle iron. You will have to experiment with how much batter makes the perfect size waffle without overflowing the sides. Everyone's waffle iron is different. Ours is a large ladle (about ½ cup) for each side (2-waffle iron)

Cook until done and brown.

Top with a beautiful poached egg, cooked bacon crumbles (leave off for vegetarian), sprinkle of parmesan cheese and some finely chopped fresh herbs such as parsley and chives. Serve and enjoy!

Need to make this gluten-free? Just omit the flour and increase the hash browns. It works!

Note: Want to know how to make the perfect poached egg to top off this recipe and the Cheesy Polenta Stack found on page 14? Here is how at the age of 58, I finally figured out how to make a beautiful poached egg. Actually, my son Aaron, taught me.

Perfect Poached Egg
1. Fill your stovetop pan ½ full of water. Add 1 Tbsp. of vinegar. Bring to a boil.
2. When you are ready to cook the egg, take a large slotted metal spoon and start spinning the water making a whirlpool vortex.
3. Gently slide your egg from a bowl into the water. The water should still be spinning. Set your timer. At the B&B, I cook the eggs for 3 minutes. At home, for some reason it takes 5 minutes. You will have to try it a few times to see how long your stove takes and how done you like your finished egg.
4. When the timer goes off, remove the egg with the slotted spoon to drain off excess water. Voila'! One pretty, perfect, poached egg!

"Not Really a Scone" Scone

I had always loved the thought of scones but couldn't stand how dry and flavorless they were. So, I set out to make a scone that is light, fluffy, and packed with lots of flavor.

Dough Ingredients
- 2 cups all-purpose flour
- ¼ cup white sugar *(you can decrease this to ⅛ cup if you want less sugar)*
- 1 Tbsp baking powder
- ½ tsp salt
- ½ cup cold unsalted butter – cut into small pieces
- ¾ cup half-n-half
- 1 tsp vanilla
- 1 large egg

Filling (here's where it gets fun!)
- 1 cup filling (fresh or frozen fruit) with 2 Tbsp sugar added as needed to taste

Over the years I have created these scones using over fifteen different combinations of fillings. Be adventurous and don't be afraid to try new options. I have included a few of my favorites at the end of this recipe.

Glaze
- 2 Tbsp butter – melted
- 3 – 5 Tbsp milk
- 1 cup powdered sugar
- ½ tsp vanilla

Instructions
1. Preheat the oven to 375°F.
2. Line a cookie sheet pan with parchment paper or a silicon mat.
3. In a large bowl, mix together the flour, sugar, baking powder, and salt.
4. Cut the butter into the flour mixture until it resembles coarse bread crumbs.

5. In a separate bowl (or glass measuring cup), whisk together the half-n-half, vanilla, and egg.
6. Stir the wet ingredients into the dry ingredients until combined. Turn out on to a lightly floured surface to finish mixing with your hands. Don't overwork – just mix. Press / roll with a rolling pin into a rectangle.
7. Spread your filling evenly across the dough and sprinkle lightly with 2 Tbsp sugar. If your filling is sweet already – such as strawberries – omit the sugar.
8. Roll the dough up tightly from the long side.
9. Slice the dough into rounds (you should get about 8 – 12) and place them on the baking tray.
10. Brush the tops of the scones with milk.
11. Bake until lightly brown. Should be about 10 minutes but watch them carefully. They are "done" when they are not gooey to the touch on the top. Allow scones to cool for at least 10 minutes before adding the glaze.
12. For the glaze: Whisk together the melted butter, milk, vanilla, and powdered sugar. Increase sugar if it needs to be thicker.
13. Once the scones are cool, drizzle with glaze and serve!

Favorite Filling Combinations:

- Peach Pie: Adding about ¼ cup of whipped cream cheese (in tiny chunks) to your fruit filling gives it a special creamy flavor. My favorite is fresh peaches straight from the orchard and a tiny dash of cinnamon.
- Blueberry – Lemon: Little Aaron's favorite is blueberry with lemon zest. Add the zest before you roll them up, then zest the tops after you add the glaze.
- Cranberry – Orange: Slice the cranberries in ½ and heat them in a bit of orange juice to make their flavor burst. Then add fresh orange zest before rolling and again after you glaze.
- Pumpkin Spice: the perfect treat on a fall morning. I use canned organic pumpkin puree, add my "pie" spices, whipped cream cheese (in tiny pieces), and roll. Add some maple syrup and spices to your glaze. Yum!
- Banana – Toasted Coconut: use up those less than pretty bananas. Mix with soft whipped cream cheese and spread on your dough. Cut, then dip both sides in coconut. The coconut toasts as the scones bake.
- Dark Chocolate with Orange: A guest suggested this flavor profile as one they had eaten in Paris. I used dark chocolate chips and the zest from a whole large orange. Watch out – these are very decedent and addictive.
- Strawberry – Rhubarb: This is the perfect early summer fruit combination. Add a bit of orange zest to boost the sweetness of the strawberries and the tartness of the rhubarb.

Make these ahead and freeze for up to one month. Just take out the quantity you want, thaw them for 30 minutes, brush with milk, and bake. Cool and add glaze drizzle.

Cheesy Polenta Stacks (Gluten-Free)

Ingredients:
- 2 cups whole milk
- 2 cups water
- 1 ½ tsp Kosher salt
- 1 cup coarse ground yellow cornmeal (polenta or grits)
- ½ tsp ground black pepper
- 4 Tbsp unsalted butter
- 4 ounces sharp Cheddar cheese, shredded
- Pesto (1 tsp per stack)
- Fresh Mozzarella slices (1 per stack)
- Fresh sliced tomato (1 per stack)
- Shredded Parmesan Cheese (1 Tbsp per stack)
- Original Mrs. Dash - herb spice mix

Start with the polenta (grits)
Place milk, water and Kosher salt into a large heavy-bottomed pot over medium heat. Bring to a boil. Stir with a whisk and gradually add yellow cornmeal (also known at polenta or grits). Once all the cornmeal has been incorporated, decrease the heat to low and cover. Remove lid and whisk/stir frequently (every 3 – 4 minutes), to prevent sticking. Cook for 20 – 25 minutes or until thick and creamy.

Remove from heat, add black pepper and unsalted butter. Stir to combine. Once the butter is melted, add Cheddar cheese. Stir until melted.

Layer stacks in this order into ramekins sprayed with cooking spray:
(I use small ramekins, but have used jelly jars as well)
1. Spoon-full of polenta
2. Pesto (I use from a jar – and just spoon it on and smear it out to the edge)
3. Slice of fresh mozzarella
4. Another spoon-full of polenta

Note: the quantities used for stacking ingredients in the ramekins depends on the size and shape of your vessels.

You can bake these now at 350°F for 45 minutes or put them in the fridge and bake them later. I make these the day before I'm going to use them for breakfast, and just pop them in the oven to bake the next morning.

To finish:
- Invert your polenta stack onto a plate or large bowl.
- Add a fresh roasted tomato slice (optional). I like to season the tomatoes with original Mrs. Dash and shredded parmesan cheese and roast them on a cookie sheet lined with foil (spray with baking spray) on 450° for 3 – 5 minutes.
- Top off with a perfect poached egg (see page 10).
- Finish with a liberal sprinkle of finely chopped herbs such as parsley, and chives, and cooked crumbled bacon (leave bacon off for vegetarian).

Spiced Chai Coffee

The perfect fit with a pumpkin spice "Not Really a Scone" scone.

Prepare your coffee maker as you normally would by filling the water tank. Before pushing the brew button add the following spices to the ground coffee in the filter:

- 1 tsp cinnamon
- ½ tsp ground cardamom
- ¼ tsp ground nutmeg
- ⅛ tsp ground ginger

Stir until mixed and continue brewing coffee according to manufacturer's directions.

This coffee is warm and inviting on a cool fall or winter morning. It also is great for an afternoon coffee over ice with some cream and sugar.

Belgium Waffle with Raspberry Sauce

Ingredients:
- 1 ½ cups all-purpose flour
- ½ cup cornstarch
- 1 tsp baking powder
- ½ tsp baking soda
- ½ tsp salt
- 1 ½ cups half-n-half *(add a dash of vinegar to make a buttermilk flavor without having to buy actual buttermilk)*
- ½ cup milk
- 6 Tbsp vegetable or canola oil
- ½ tsp vanilla extract
- 2 large eggs, white and yolks separated
- 3 Tbsp white granulated sugar

Preheat oven to 200°F. Preheat waffle iron (it's OK if your iron is not a Belgian waffle maker). In a mixing bowl whisk flour, cornstarch, baking powder, baking soda and salt. Make a well in the center – set aside.

In a separate mixing bowl combine half-n-half, milk, vegetable oil, vanilla extract, and egg yolks.

In your mixer bowl, whip egg whites until soft peaks form. Add sugar and whip until stiff glossy peaks form.

Pour milk mixture into the well in your flour mixture and combine. Batter will be slightly lumpy. Gently fold in the egg white mixture. Cook in waffle iron according to manufacturer's directions. Once each waffle is done, transfer to warm oven and allow to rest until crisp. This way you can make waffles for a crowd and serve when ready. You can serve these with butter and syrup or with fresh fruit and lightly sweetened fresh whipped cream. European style! We serve our waffles with European whipped cream and raspberry sauce. (page 18)

Raspberry Sauce

The perfect complement to the Belgium Waffles on page 17.

Ingredients:
- 4 tsp cornstarch
- ½ cup sugar
- 1 ½ cups raspberries, fresh or frozen
- 1 ½ tsp water
- 1 ½ tsp lemon juice
- 1 Tbsp butter
- ½ tsp vanilla
- Dash salt

Process:
1. Put cornstarch in a medium sized sauce pan.
2. Add sugar and stir ingredients together.
3. Add water and lemon juice. Stir to combine. It will look pasty.
4. Add raspberries. If using frozen – semi-thaw in microwave first to break them apart). Stir gently so the berries are coated and start to break down.
5. Bring the mixture to a boil over medium heat, stirring frequently. Let it simmer for 1 minute. It should thicken into a nice syrup consistency.
6. Remove from the heat and add butter, vanilla and dash of salt.
7. Serve over waffles with some lightly sweetened heavy whipped cream.

We put this in a small crock pot until ready to serve at breakfast. If you need to thin it at all, add a tiny bit of orange juice.

Beautiful and yummy. I have also made this with other fruit like huckleberries or strawberries.

Inspired by Jamie Cooks

Aaron's Mushroom Gravy with Biscuits

Aaron created this recipe one weekend when he and Lindsey came home for a visit. It is all vegetarian and totally yummy (even if you are a meat lover).

Ingredients
- 1 onion
- 6 Tbsp oil
- 8 cloves garlic
- 20 oz fresh mushrooms
- 6 Tbsp butter
- 8 Tbsp flour
- 2 cups veggie broth
- 2 Tbsp soy sauce
- 4 tsp salt
- 2 tsp black pepper
- 2 tsp smoked paprika
- 4 cups milk

Directions
1. Dice onion and add to pan with oil on medium high heat. Cook until onions start to brown.
2. Dice mushrooms and garlic and add to the pan with onions. Continue cooking until mushrooms start to brown and soften.
3. Add butter to pan and melt. Stir in flour when butter is melted and begins to bubble. Cook for a couple of minutes until flour and mushroom mixture starts to stick to the bottom of the pan.
4. Combine veggie broth, soy sauce, salt, pepper, and paprika. Add to pan to deglaze. Stir to incorporate flour mixture and liquid.
5. Bring to a boil and add milk. Reduce heat to medium low and stir occasionally until you reach your desired thickness.

Mushroom Selection: Always use fresh mushrooms, but you can vary the type to give different flavors to the gravy. Cremini mushrooms give a rich, earthy taste similar to beef gravy. Oyster mushrooms are more delicate and make a good chicken or turkey gravy substitute, especially if you throw in a little turmeric and nutritional yeast with the spice mixture. Shitake mushrooms have a rich, smoky taste making them a good substitute for pork sausage, especially when mixed with a teaspoon of maple syrup and some fresh minced sage. If all you have is white button mushrooms, don't worry, you can still make a great gravy. Play around with adding some additional spice such as cayenne or mixing in some fresh herbs such as thyme, sage, or rosemary.

Dinner Gravy
This gravy can be used for any recipe, but a dinner gravy usually has less or no milk. You can omit the milk and replace it with more veggie broth plus a couple of tablespoons of red wine for a great tasting gravy to use on mashed potatoes or roasted veggies. You may need to add a bit more flour or an additional thickener such as cornstarch to get the consistency you want.

Vegan Option
I quite often use unsweetened cashew or almond milk instead of cow's milk and you can use vegan margarine instead of butter. You may need to play around with adding additional thickener as this can sometimes change the texture a bit.

Gluten Free / Soy Free
You can use gluten free flour to thicken, but maybe play around with it first to see if it thickens property. To eliminate the soy sauce (which typically has gluten), add a tablespoon of molasses and a tablespoon of red wine.

Biscuits Not from a Box or Can

Makes 8 – 10 biscuits
Ingredients:
- 2 cups all-purpose flour
- 2 ½ tsp baking powder
- ½ tsp cream of tartar
- ½ tsp salt
- ⅓ cup shortening
- ¾ cup milk

Biscuits Prep and Bake
Preheat oven to 475°F. Stir together dry ingredients. Cut in shortening. Add milk and mix. Put onto a floured surface and knead with your hands until combined and smooth. Roll out to ¾". Cut with biscuit cutter. Place close together on a greased baking sheet or 9x13. Bake at 475°F for 11-15 minutes.

David's All Meat Gravy with Biscuits

Many sausage gravy recipes start with a basic white gravy then add the sausage. Dave's secret is to start with the sausage and then make the gravy. For maximum flavor, cook over the campfire in a cast iron Dutch oven. ☺

1. Brown your choice of finely ground breakfast sausage. (1 – 16 oz. tube of Jimmy Dean's)
2. Add ½ cup of flour and brown, making a roux. Depending on how lean your sausage is, you may have to add additional butter.
3. Add your choice of spices – anything will work – salt, pepper and original Mrs. Dash herb blend are some of David's favorites.
4. Add two cups of milk or half-n-half and bring to a boil to thicken.
5. Reduce heat and simmer, adding more milk to desired consistency. You will want your gravy a little thinner than you think at this point since it will thicken as it cools.

6. If you end up with gravy that is too thin, simply mix cold milk and flour – start with about a Tbsp of flour to ½ cup of milk – add and reheat.

The nice thing about gravy is that it can be extended to almost any quantity you want – just don't dilute your sausage too much or you lose that rich meaty flavor.

When cooking biscuits and gravy for the B&B, we prepare the gravy, then place it in a small crock pot to simmer. It's ready to serve with freshly baked biscuits. Perfect breakfast for a blustery fall morning.

Some of the best food is cooked over an open fire.

Easy Overnight Cinnamon Rolls

Make and bake, or make and save, or make and freeze. Always fresh, hot and sweet! This traditional American roll is a throw-back to David's mom who loved to serve cinnamon rolls on Sunday morning.

Dough:
- 1 cup milk
- ¼ cup warm water
- 1 tsp vanilla extract
- ½ cup butter
- 2 eggs – room temperature (If you forgot to get them out earlier, just put them in a bowl of hot tap water to sit while you prep everything else)
- ½ tsp salt
- ½ cup white sugar
- 5 cups all-purpose flour
- 1 Tbsp vital wheat gluten
- 3 tsp instant active dry yeast

Cinnamon Filling
- ½ cup butter – melted
- ½ cup firmly packed brown sugar
- ½ cup white sugar
- 4 tsp cinnamon

Process
1. Put milk, water, and butter in a microwave safe measuring cup and heat until butter starts to melt, and milk is warm.
2. Add yeast and allow to sit while you combine other ingredients (except flour) in your mixer bowl with dough hook.
3. Add yeast milk mixture to other ingredients. Now – add the flour last.
4. Knead in mixer for 10 minutes. Dough should be smooth, elastic, and silky looking, and springs back when poked with lightly with your finger.
5. Cover the bowl with plastic wrap and allow to rise until

double in size (approximately 1 hour)

6. Spray your baking pans with non-stick cooking spray. 1 – 9x13 or several smaller ones as desired. If I'm going to freeze these I use inexpensive aluminum pans with lids or large flat plastic containers with lids.
7. After the dough has risen, place it on a floured surface and roll out to approximately a 15 x 24 inch rectangle. It is very elastic, so take your time and stretch it out as you go.
8. Brush dough with melted butter spreading it all the way to the edges. Sprinkle the entire surface with the cinnamon filling.
9. Starting with the long edge, roll up the dough and pinch seams to seal. Note: rolling too tight will result in the center of your rolls popping up and out.
10. With a pastry cutter, mark off 1 ½" sections. Cut. Place rolls cut side up in the pan. They should not touch each other before rising.

Baking Immediately:
Cover pan and let rolls rise for 1 hour or until doubled. Preheat oven to 350°F. Bake approximately 20 – 25 minutes until light brown. Remove from oven and glaze with butter glaze from the scone recipe (page 11).

Make and Refrigerate:
Place rolls in a pan. Cover with plastic wrap and set in refrigerator overnight (or up to 2 days). Before baking, allow rolls to rise for 30 - 60 minutes.

Make and Freeze:
Rolls can be placed in the pan, covered, and frozen for up to 1 month. Before baking, allow rolls to thaw OVERNIGHT on the counter (or refrigerator) and then follow normal instructions for baking.

Note: I always keep a pan of these in our freezer. It works great if David or Rachel end up doing breakfast without me. These rolls are not overly sweet, which we like. Who doesn't love a fresh – hot – gooey cinnamon roll?

Gluten-Free Breakfast Danish

Don't let the word gluten-free scare you from trying these traditional pastry rolls. They are yummy!

Ingredients:
- 2 ¼ tsp (1 packet) yeast
- ¼ cup HOT tap water
- 3 cups Bob's Red Mill Gluten-Free 1 to 1 Baking Flour
- 1 Tbsp baking powder
- 4 Tbsp butter *(use shortening if you need dairy free)*
- 1 ¼ cups liquid whey or half-n-half or a combination of both (use orange juice if you need dairy free)
- 1 egg *(use ¼ cup of applesauce if you need vegan)*
- ½ tsp vanilla extract
- 1 ½ - 2 cups fruit jam *(use sugar -free if needed)*
- 1 ½ - 2 cups whipped cream cheese

Glaze – use butter glaze from scone recipe on page 11

Instructions:

1. Preheat oven to 400°F. Prepare baking pan with spray, parchment paper, or silicon mat.
2. Add yeast to hot tap water and set aside for 5 minutes.
3. Mix together flour and baking powder in mixing bowl.
4. Cut in butter *(or shortening)* till it resembles small peas
5. In a separate bowl, combine yeast/water, whey (half-n-half or orange juice), egg and vanilla
6. Combine liquid and dry ingredients and mix by hand. It will start out looking too wet, then combine into a smooth dough.
7. Dust your hands with gluten-free flour. Take a big spoonful of dough and roll it into a ball. It should be the size of a kiwi. Set these on your baking sheet.
8. Find an object – like a glass jar – to use as a "press". Dip the bottom of your pressing jar in flour, then gently press down on the ball spreading them out and leaving your edge and the well in the center.
9. Using a teaspoon, create a nice size rounded spoonful of whipped cream cheese. Drop these in the center of each pastry.
10. Use another teaspoon and add jam to the center of each roll.
11. Bake in pre-heated oven for 10 – 12 minutes or until edges are golden brown and dough is cooked. Allow to cool.
12. Drizzle glaze in a cross-hatch pattern across each roll. Leave off glaze if you need sugar-free.
13. Place on your favorite decorative serving platter and watch your guests' mouths' drop when you tell them these are gluten-free. Makes about 12 – 15 rolls depending on how big you make the dough balls.

Baked Egg Cassoulet

Regularly featured on our B&B breakfast menu. We make this in individual, decorative ramekins sprayed with cooking spray. They can be made the day before and put in the fridge until you're ready to start breakfast. Makes 4 – 6 ramekins depending on their size and how much you put in each. This cassoulet can be made gluten-free.

Ingredients:

- ¾ - 1 cup of diced French bread **per ramekin** (we use left over brötchen rolls from breakfast.) *For gluten-free, substitute frozen shredded hash browns.*
- 2 Tbsp each (**per ramekin**) of fresh diced/chopped vegetables or meat that you want to use. Cooked bacon or ham, green onions, sweet peppers, fresh mushrooms or fresh spinach are all good choices.
- 2 – 4 Tbsp shredded cheddar cheese per ramekin
- ¼ cup butter
- 2 cups milk
- 6 eggs
- 1 Tbsp Mrs. Dash spice blend
- 1 tsp salt
- ½ tsp ground black pepper
- 1 Tbsp dry mustard
- 1 tsp fine Italian herbs

Process:

1. Spray your ramekins with cooking spray and set them on a foil lined baking sheet. Add the diced bread, dividing it equally between dishes to make the quantity you desire. You want the level of the bread cubes to come just below the top rim of the ramekin. For gluten-free, substitute frozen shredded hash browns.
- Add the diced meat and vegetables to the bread. Add the shredded Cheddar cheese next. "Fluff" this mixture with your hands to toss it all together and set aside.
- Melt butter in a large measuring bowl. Add milk, and

eggs. Whisk until well combined.

- Add mustard, salt, pepper and spices into your milk mixture. Whisk.
- Slowly pour the egg/milk mixture over the top of the ingredients in the ramekins. Press down to soak bread cubes in liquid. Add more as needed. If you run out before the ramekins are full, just top them off with some extra milk.
- Cover them with saran wrap and set them in the fridge until the next morning.
- When ready to bake, preheat oven to 375° – 400° F. Put the tray with ramekins in the oven and bake for 1 hour. They are done when puffed up and springy in the center. Be prepared for some "ooohhs and ahhhs" as you pull these out of the oven. They are truly beautiful. Serve immediately.

Hot from the oven.

Roasted Pears with Goat Cheese and Bacon

This recipe was created to utilize an over-abundant harvest of pears from our B&B tree. It can be adjusted for vegetarian or dairy free.

Ingredients:
- You will need ½ pear for each person. The pears should be fresh, but not over-ripe or too soft.
- Goat Cheese crumbles
- Bacon
- Course Sea Salt
- Honey

Process:
1. Preheat oven to 400°F.
2. Wash and cut the pears in half and set them in a baking dish lined with foil.
3. Scoop out the core leaving a cavity in the center of each half. I use a small melon baller for this job.
4. Add 1 Tbsp of goat cheese crumbles to the inside cavity of each pear. For dairy free – fill cavity with chopped pecan pieces.
5. Wrap each pear half in 1 slice of bacon (not thick cut). You may need to secure the end with a toothpick depending on the size of your pear and the length of the bacon slice. Leave off bacon for vegetarian option.
6. Bake for approximately 1 hour.
7. Remove from oven, drizzle with honey, and sprinkle with sea salt.
8. Enjoy! The perfect combination of sweet, smoky and salty.

Stuffed Breakfast Mushrooms

Who doesn't love stuffed mushrooms! Most people think of this for a dinner appetizer, but we love to add it to our breakfast buffet.

Ingredients – Quantity varies based on number of mushrooms:
- Medium – large fresh button mushrooms (approximately 10 – 12)
- Whipped Cream Cheese (approximately 2 cups)
- Italian Bread crumbs (approximately 1/3 cup)
- Shredded parmesan cheese (approximately ¼ cup)
- Fresh parsley (approximately 3 Tbsp)
- Fresh chives (approximately 3 Tbsp)
- Bacon – cooked and diced (optional) (approximately 6 Tbsp)

Process
1. Preheat the oven to 350°F, and line a baking dish with foil sprayed with cooking spray.
2. Wipe the mushrooms with a dry paper towel, then remove the stems.
3. In a bowl, mix together whipped cream cheese, Italian breadcrumbs, fresh herbs, shredded parmesan cheese, and bacon if using.
4. Stuff the mushrooms with the cheese mixture and place in the baking dish.
5. Bake for 20 minutes.
6. Serve hot!

Gluten-Free Blueberry Muffins

Gluten-free does not have to mean flavorless when it comes to this muffin recipe. It can also be made sugar-free and dairy-free.

Ingredients:
- 2 cups Bob's Red Mill Gluten-Free 1 to 1 Baking Flour
- 2 tsp baking powder
- ½ tsp salt
- ½ cup unsalted butter *(use shortening for dairy-free)*
- 1 ¼ cups sugar (+ 2 tsp) *(sub ¼ cup agave nectar for sugar-free)*
- 2 eggs
- ½ cup buttermilk (or milk with a dash of vinegar or lemon juice) *(substitute applesauce for dairy-free)*
- 1 ½ cups fresh or frozen blueberries *(or huckleberries)*

Steps:
1. Preheat oven to 425°F. Spray muffin pan with nonstick spray or line with paper baking cups. I use lightly sprayed paper baking cups.
2. Whisk together flour, baking powder, and salt. Set aside.
3. In your mixer bowl, cream together butter and the 1 ¼ cup sugar until light and fluffy, about 10 minutes, scraping the bowl often. Add eggs one at a time, beating well after each.
4. Add half of the flour mixture and beat until blended. Beat in the buttermilk, and then add remaining flour mixture and beat until fully blended. Gently fold the blueberries into the batter.
5. Spoon batter evenly into 12 baking cups. Sprinkle the tops with the 2 tsp of sugar (optional)
6. Tap the pan lightly on the counter-top a couple of times to release any air bubbles in the batter. Place pan in oven and immediately reduce heat to 375. Bake for 20 minutes or until muffin tops are golden brown. Test with toothpick for doneness. Cool for 5 minutes and serve.

David's Easy Blueberry Oatmeal Muffins

When I have a breakfast off, David loves to make these fresh, yummy blueberry muffins for our guests.

Ingredients:
- 2 eggs
- 3/4 – 1 cup Fresh or frozen blueberries
- 2/3 cup brown sugar
- ½ cup vegetable oil
- ½ cup milk
- 1 cup flour
- ¾ cup oatmeal (not quick)
- 1 tsp baking powder
- ½ tsp baking soda
- 1 pinch salt

Directions:
1. Preheat oven to 400°F.
2. Grease / spray 12 muffin cups. We like to use paper liners as well.
3. Whisk eggs, brown sugar, vegetable oil, and milk together in a bowl until smooth.
4. Stir in flour, oatmeal, baking powder, baking soda, and salt into wet ingredients to form a batter. Add the blueberries.
5. Fill the prepared muffin cups with batter.
6. Bake in preheated oven until tops are golden brown and a toothpick comes out clean – about 20 minutes.

Grandson "little Aaron" picking wild huckleberries.

Breakfast Crock-pot Applesauce

We put this in the crock-pot the night before and let it cook overnight. We then have wonderful, hot, sweet, fresh applesauce to serve with breakfast the next morning...and the guests get to smell it cooking all night.

Feel free to vary this depending on your fruit and how sweet you like your applesauce.

- 20 apples – cleaned, cored and chopped
- 1 ½ cups sugar (you can use a combination of white and brown, depending on what you like)
- 2 Tbsp lemon juice
- 2 Tbsp cinnamon or pumpkin pie spice

Put all your ingredients together in your crockpot and cook overnight on low.

In the morning, you can further mash up your apples by using a hand mixer or leave them chunky.

This is a delicious way to warm up the morning on a cold winter day.

Zwiebelkuchen
German Onion Cake (Tart)

This traditional German quiche-like tart is served with fresh-

pressed wine at the beginning of the fall wine harvest. The host at our little pension on the Moselle River made this cake for us, then walked to the near-by vineyard and brought back a 5-gallon open bucket of  "fresh" wine to drink with this savory treat.

We made this as mini-tarts for our Oktoberfest celebration. My grandson LOVES the Onion Cake. Don't be afraid – it is so good. Just be prepared for some tears. It takes lots and lots of caramelized onions.

Crust:
- 1 tsp yeast
- ⅓ cup of warm milk
- ½ cup + 2 Tbsp of flour
- ½ tsp salt
- 4 Tbsp butter (room temp – cut into small pieces).

Dissolve yeast in warm milk. Let it stand for 5 minutes. Combine flour and salt and in a bowl. Add butter and use a pastry cutter to combine well. Add the milk mixture. Using a dough hook or food processor, knead for 6 minutes. Add more milk or flour as needed to form dough ball. Put into a small bowl sprayed with cooking spray and cover loosely with plastic wrap. Let rise in a warm place until doubled in size (1 hour).

Onion/bacon mixture:
- 5 slices of bacon (finely diced)
- 2 Tbsp butter
- 2 ¼ pounds yellow onions (finely diced).

Fry the bacon until done in a large heavy skillet or sauce pan. Add the butter to the bacon and throw in the diced onions. Reduce the heat and let the onions slowly caramelize to a nice golden brown (about 30 minutes). Remove from the heat and allow to cool.

Filling:
- 1 ½ cups full fat sour cream
- 4 eggs
- 2 Tbsp flour
- 1 tsp salt
- Pepper to taste

In a bowl combine the sour cream, eggs, flour, salt, and pepper. Mix well. Add to the onion/bacon mixture and combine thoroughly.

To finish:
Break off 6 small balls of dough. Roll out thin and line a small tart pan, sprayed with cooking spray, making a rustic edge crust. Evenly distribute the filling between the six tarts.

Bake on the middle rack for 45 minutes in a 400° F oven, until the top is light brown and the center feels firm to the touch. Let cool for 15 minutes and then pop them out of your tart pans before serving.

You can make the dough and the onion mixture the night before to save time. Wrap the dough in plastic wrap or zip-lock bag. Tightly cover the onion mixture. Then it's all ready to finish up in the morning.

Connie's Note added June 2018: To achieve the optimum enjoyment out of creating such a wonderful German delicacy, add the perfect young German couple from Darmstadt, a bottle of Riesling, and a warm summer night. The two+ pounds of onions you have to peel and chop will be done in no-time. Florian and Christina, I will think of you and your visit to the B&B every time I make this. ☺

Asparagus Goat Cheese Quiche

Since the crust for this quiche is actually cooked rice, it makes the perfect gluten-free option. I like this with fresh asparagus, green onions, and goat cheese, but you can vary the vegetables, meat and cheese to fit your taste and what's available for the growing season.

Ingredients:
- 2 cups cooked rice (white or brown – don't overcook)
- 2 egg whites
- ½ cup shredded cheddar cheese – for crust
- Salt and pepper to taste
- 1Tbsp ground mustard
- 2 cups fresh asparagus
- ½ cup green onions – sliced/diced
- ¼ cup cooked and crumbled bacon (optional)
- 4 oz crumbled goat cheese
- 5 eggs
- 1 ½ cups milk
- 1 ½ cups shredded cheddar cheese – for filling

Directions:
1. Mix cooked rice, lightly beaten egg whites, and shredded cheese in a large bowl.
2. Grease a 10" oven-safe skillet, pie, or casserole dish. Add the rice mixture, pressing down to pack it tightly on the bottom and up the sides, forming a pie-like crust.
3. Bake at 375° F for 15 minutes. Cool slightly.
4. Once the rice crust has baked and cooled, spread half of the cheddar cheese along the bottom of the crust. Arrange your vegetables and bacon on top of the cheese. Add the goat cheese crumbles, and top with the remaining cheese.
5. Combine eggs, milk, mustard, salt and pepper to taste and whisk until frothy. Pour egg mixture on top of the vegetables in the crust.
6. Bake for 40 – 50 minutes at 350° F or until a knife inserted in the center comes out clean.
7. Let it cool for at least 10 minutes before serving.

2 LUNCH

We don't typically serve lunch at the B&B, but over the past few years we had developed and utilized several key lunch recipes for special events and box lunch deliveries.

When I think of lunch from my childhood, it most commonly relates to some type of sandwich. I remember one time, I think I was about eight or ten years old, my mom went to an appointment and my older sister and I were home alone. She was late, so she called us to ask us to make her a sandwich and deliver it to her. She asked for peanut butter and mayonnaise. We said yes, then hung up the phone. Immediately an argument ensued. Did she really say peanut butter and mayo? How could that be? No one eats mayo with their peanut butter. Finally, we just made it and set out on our bikes to deliver it to mom. And yes, that is truly what she ordered.

When we travel in Europe, we often gather our lunch needs from the local open-air market. We stop at the meat booth and get some salami, visit the bakery for fresh rolls, and finish our lunch off with cheese and fruit. This goes in our day-bag and is usually eaten at a road-side picnic area somewhere along the way.

Now, lunch time is usually a bit of a running scavenger hunt. Grabbing something here and there to tie us over until dinner time. Might be some cheese and crackers with fresh fruit or left-over baked eggs and fruit.

Hopefully you can use these recipes in this chapter for lunch, but don't be afraid to save them for dinner as well.

Broccoli Salad

Makes about 6 servings as a great compliment to a sandwich. I've never been a huge fan of raw broccoli, but a friend brought this salad to a church women's event, and I fell in love. It has now become a key component of our box lunch orders.

Ingredients:
1 – head fresh broccoli, cut into bite size pieces
½ cup dried cranberries
¼ cup red onion, finely chopped
2 Tbsp white sugar
3 Tbsp white wine vinegar
1 cup mayonnaise
1 cup sunflower seeds
10 slices bacon

Directions:
1. Place bacon in a large, deep skillet. Cook until evenly brown. (We cook our bacon in the oven on a sheet pan with foil – 350 for about 20+ minutes). Crumble and set aside.
2. In a salad bowl, toss together broccoli, cranberries, and red onions. In a separate bowl, whisk together the white sugar, vinegar, and mayonnaise. Pour over broccoli mixture and toss to coat. Refrigerate for at least 2 hours.
3. Before serving, sprinkle with sunflower seeds and crumbled bacon. Toss and serve.

Inspired by allrecipes.com

Afternoon European Ice Coffee

This is the perfect way to use left over coffee brewed in the morning. In Germany / Austria, everyone stops for afternoon coffee, cake and a little break about 2:00 p.m. When I make this on a hot summer afternoon, it brings back so many memories. Don't have left-over coffee? Just brew a new cup and let it cool. It's totally worth the effort.

- Fill a tall beverage glass with ice.
- Add coffee leaving 1" – 2" at the top (depending on how much cream or half-n-half you like)
- Add several teaspoons of sugar to taste. Stir.
- Add 1/2 tsp of vanilla. Stir.
- Fill to the top with milk product of your choice. Cream, half-n-half, whole milk or almond milk. Stir.
- Add whip cream (I keep a can in the fridge just for this purpose).
- Sprinkle whip cream with some cinnamon.
- Add a comfy chair, a soft purring cat, an afternoon breeze and enjoy.

Hungarian Mushroom Soup

This warm, rich vegetarian soup goes great with a grilled cheese sandwich or salad. Serve it for lunch or dinner.

Ingredients:
   2 Tbsp butter
   1 large onion, diced
   1 clove garlic, minced
   12 oz fresh mushrooms (cremini or white button) chopped
   2 Tbsp paprika
   4 tsp fresh dill, chopped (or 2 tsp dried dill)
   2 tsp salt
   1 tsp pepper
   1 tsp smoked paprika
   ¼ tsp cayenne
   3 Tbsp butter
   2 Tbsp flour
   1 cup milk
   2 cups beef or vegetable broth
   1 Tbsp soy sauce
   ½ cup sour cream
   Fresh parsley – chopped for garnish
   Sour cream – for garnish

Directions:
1. Melt 2 Tbsp butter in small pan. Sauté the onions until translucent and just beginning to brown. Add garlic and sauté for another minute. Add mushrooms and sauté for 5 minutes until the mushrooms release their juices. Add spices. Set aside.
2. In cast iron skillet, melt 3 Tbsp butter and stir in the flour, constantly whisking for several minutes until the mixture is a rich caramelized brown. Add the milk, broth, and soy sauce, whisking until the mixture is smooth. Add the mushroom mixture. Bring to boil, reduce heat to medium, cover and simmer for 15 minutes, stirring occasionally. Stir in the sour cream, simmer for another 2 minutes.
3. Serve immediately with garnish. Great with rustic bread.

Chocolate Chip Cookies

Every guest that stays at the Husum Riverside Bed & Breakfast finds homemade cookies waiting when they check-in. Most of the time these are Chocolate Chip. Consequently, I make/bake over 1000 cookies a year. My trick? I always make a double batch. I use an ice cream scoop to put the unbaked cookie dough "balls" on a large sheet pan. Then I put them in the freezer for 24 hours. When frozen, I remove them and put them in a storage tub. They will keep in the freezer for three months. Now, when I need a few cookies, I just take out what I need, let them thaw for 20 minutes and bake. Fresh, hot, delicious chocolate chip cookies. The only problem is to keep them from being discovered by those in the family who like to eat frozen cookie dough ☺

Ingredients:
- 2 ¼ cups all-purpose flour
- 1 tsp baking soda
- 1 tsp salt
- 1 cup shortening
- ¾ cup granulated sugar
- ¾ cup light brown sugar
- 1 tsp vanilla extract
- 2 large eggs
- 1 ½ cups semi-sweet chocolate chips

Process:
1. Preheat oven to 375° F.
2. Combine flour, baking soda, and salt in a small bowl. Set aside.
3. In your mixer bowl, beat shortening, granulated sugar, brown sugar and vanilla extract until creamy.
4. Add eggs (one at a time), beating well after each addition.
5. Gradually beat in the flour mixture.
6. Stir in 1 ½ cups semi-sweet chocolate chips.
7. Drop by rounded tablespoons (I use the ice cream scoop method) onto an ungreased baking sheet lined

with parchment paper.
8. Bake for 8 – 10 minutes. I tend to not "over-bake" my cookies. They will continue to bake a bit after they are removed from the oven. I like them a bit soft, chewy, and not overly brown.
9. Cool for five minutes, then remove and continue to cool on wire racks. Enjoy!

Makes 3 – 5 dozen depending on how large you make them.

Inspired by Original Toll House Chocolate Chip Cookies

Pumpkin and Black Bean Soup

Pumpkin soup, known as Kürbissuppe, is very popular in Germany during the fall months. It was one of David's favorite things to order when we traveled in Germany. We created this soup recipe to offer our guests staying during the cold fall and winter months. It freezes great in individual serving containers and can quickly be thawed, heated and served with a semmel and fresh fruit for a quick, late-night supper. Room service anyone?

Ingredients:
2 Tbsp olive oil
1 medium onion, finely chopped
3 cups of canned or packaged vegetable stock
1 – 14 ½ oz can diced tomatoes in juice
1 – 15 oz can black beans, drained
1 – 15 oz can pumpkin puree (not pumpkin pie filling)
1 cup heavy cream
1 Tbsp curry powder
1 ½ tsp ground cumin
½ tsp cayenne pepper
2 tsp salt
Fresh chives for garnish

Directions:
Heat soup pot over medium heat – then add oil. When oil is hot, add onion and sauté for 5 minutes. Add broth, tomatoes, black beans, and pumpkin puree. Stir to combine and bring to a boil. Reduce heat to medium low and stir in cream, curry, cumin, cayenne, and salt. Simmer for 5 minutes. Garnish with chives and serve.

Inspired by www.kitchme.com

Pesto Panini

This sandwich was one of our best sellers in the summer restaurant! Don't despair if you don't have a panini maker, just heat a skillet, put in your sandwich, cover with a smaller lid, weigh it down with a few cans of food, and you've got yourself a home-made panini press. A good friend wanted to be sure I didn't forget to include this recipe in the cookbook. This one's for you, Wendy!

Ingredients:
- Pesto
- Black olives - chopped
- Tomatoes - thinly sliced
- Sharp Cheddar Cheese – thinly sliced
- Rustic French bread – sliced, but not too thin

For each Sandwich:
1. Spread pesto on one side of each piece of your sandwich bread. It should be covered but not thick.
2. Place a thin layer of olives on one slice of the bread. Covering bread, but not in heavy layers or chunks.
3. Place 3 – 4 tomato slices on top of the olives. They can be slightly overlapped, but still inside the edges of the bread.
4. Place cheese on top of the tomatoes (about 1 – 2 full sized slices). Tear and rearrange as needed so they don't overlap.
5. Place top piece of bread on the cheese and lightly brush both sides with olive oil. DO NOT SOAK.
6. Place on pre-heated (425°F) Panini press with the cheese side on the top so that it melts down. Close the press. Cook until grill lines are dark brown, and the rest of the sandwich is golden brown. The cheese should be melted. Remove from the press using a wood utensil, cut in ½, serve immediately.

Bacon, Brie and Berry Panini

Adjust ingredients depending on the number of sandwiches you are making. See note on page 46 if you don't have a panini press.

Ingredients:
- Bacon / cooked – but not crisp or it will crumble in the panini press
- Brie – sliced
- Blackberry Dijon mustard (or similar – just not yellow)
- Marionberry peach jam (or something similar – we use Apple Valley Jam from Hood River, Oregon. Berry based jams are what makes the best flavor profile)
- Rustic French Bread

For each sandwich:
1. Spread mustard on one side of the bread and the jam on the other. Aaron usually built from the mustard side up.
2. Place thinly sliced brie. Cover entire surface of bread slice without overlapping.
3. Cover cheese with 2 full pieces of bacon. Try not to overlap / Aaron placed them at an angle to make it easier to cut the sandwich after it is cooked.
4. Place top piece of bread over the bacon and brush both outsides with olive oil. DO NOT SOAK.
5. Place on a pre-heated (425°F) panini press with the cheese side on the top. Close and cook until grill lines are dark brown, and the rest of the sandwich is golden brown.
6. Use a wood utensil to remove – without scratching the panini press. Cut in ½ and serve immediately.

Chicken Corn Chowder

This was very popular in our little restaurant. Aaron and Lindsey also served this for the soup buffet at their wedding.

Ingredients:

- 3 cups chicken meat, cooked and shredded
- 8 slices bacon, cooked and crumbled
- ¼ cup butter, diced into 1 tbsp pieces
- 1 large red bell pepper, diced (1 1/2 cups)
- 1 medium yellow onion, diced (1 1/4 cups)
- 1 – 2 jalapenos, seeded for less heat, finely chopped
- 4 cloves garlic, minced
- ⅓ cup flour
- 6 cups low-sodium chicken broth
- 3 medium russet potatoes, peeled and diced (3 cups)
- 2 bay leaves
- Salt and pepper to taste
- 2 ½ cups frozen or fresh corn
- 1 ½ cups half-n-half
- Green onions – for garnish – optional

Directions:

1. In a large pot, melt butter over medium heat. Add red bell pepper, onions, and jalapenos and sauté until tender – about 3 minutes. Add garlic and cook 30 seconds longer.
2. Stir in flour, and cook 2 minutes, stirring constantly. While stirring, slowly add in the chicken broth and whisk until well blended.
3. Add potatoes, and bay leaves and season with salt, and pepper to taste. Bring mixture to a boil, stirring frequently. Then reduce heat to medium-low and cook, uncovered for 10 minutes or until potatoes are tender. Stir occasionally.
4. Add in cooked chicken, corn, and half-n-half. Simmer uncovered 10 – 15 minutes longer, stirring occasionally.
5. Serve warm, topped with bacon and green onions.

Inspired by Better Homes and Gardens / cookingclassy.com

Summer Sparkling Lemonade

There is nothing like a cool, fresh citrus drink over ice on a hot summer day. The bubbling, sparkling mineral water is just a bonus.

Ingredients:
- 5 ½ lemons (squeeze and strain out seeds)
- ¼ cup granulated sugar
- Splash of boiling water (just enough to dissolve sugar)
- ⅓ cup of sparkling mineral water
- Ice
- Lemon slices to garnish

Directions:
1. Dissolve sugar with the boiling water in a pan. Cool.
2. Add lemon juice to sugar water. Cool.
3. Fill a tall glass with ice.
4. Put ½ cup of lemon/sugar syrup in glass.
5. Fill remaining glass with sparkling water.
6. Garnish with lemon slice.

Once you have made this, you can adjust the quantities of lemon-sugar syrup to sparkling water to your own personal taste. You can also add a few fresh strawberries or raspberries. This will save in the fridge for several days.

3 DINNER

With our kids growing up at home, dinner was always the time that we came together to share about our day, enjoy good food, and begin to wind down as we headed into the evening. Sometimes, dinner might be at noon, like on Sunday after church. Other times, it was early in the evening, so we could get the kids to whatever evening event was on the schedule. Personally, what I love about dinner, is that, even if for just a little while, we are all gathered around the table together. Everything else stops. It's family time.

Most of the recipes in the dinner section are attributed to Aaron and were created by him during the time we had a little weekend evening restaurant going on. Some were created specifically for a special event or dinner; others were community favorites that people ordered over and over.

I never ceased to be amazed at how Aaron could take ingredients he brought home from the farmer's market, put them together with some unique flavoring from his massive spice collection, and prepare such wonderful plates of food. His goal was to create great, fresh food at a super price that anyone and everyone could come, sit on the patio in the warm evening sun, and enjoy.

Burgers and Homemade Brioche Buns

Our goal with all food prepared at the Bed & Breakfast is to have it be fresh and homemade, including the hamburger buns.

Icehouse Burger:

Ingredients (for 3 – 4 burgers):
- 1 lb. lean hamburger
- 3 Tbsp red wine
- 1 tsp Worcestershire sauce
- 1 tsp salt
- 1 tsp pepper
- ¾ cup shitake mushrooms
- 10 oz soft goat cheese
- 1 cup of olive oil mayonnaise
- ¼ tsp black pepper
- ¼ tsp kosher salt
- 1 Tbsp finely chopped fresh thyme

Process:
1. Marinate hamburger meat with red wine, Worcestershire sauce, salt and black pepper. Form patties to your desired thickness. Cook to desired level of doneness.
2. Sauté' finely chopped shitake mushrooms in olive oil. Set aside.
3. Make goat cheese-thyme-mayo spread by combining goat cheese, olive oil mayonnaise, black pepper, kosher salt, and fresh thyme.
4. Assemble burger on the bun with cooked patty, goat cheese spread, mushrooms, and lettuce.

Lindsey Burger: for vegetarian option, replace the meat with a marinated Portobello mushroom. (Aaron created this for his sweetie, Lindsey.)

Brioche Burger Buns:

Ingredients:
- 1 ¼ cup warm milk
- 2 Tbsp yeast
- 2 Tbsp sugar
- 1/3 cup melted butter
- 1 large egg
- 3 ¼ cups flour
- 1 tsp salt
- 1 egg for egg wash
- Poppy seeds or sesame seeds

Process:
1. Preheat oven to 425°F. Line baking sheet with parchment paper.
2. In the mixer bowl, gently stir together warm milk, yeast, sugar, melted butter and large egg.
3. Add in flour, and salt. Mix with the paddle attachment on low until combined. Then switch to the dough hook and knead on low for 5 – 7 minutes. Dough should be smooth and elastic, but not wet and sticky.
4. Divide the dough into about 12 pieces and shape each one into a ball. Place dough balls on baking sheet 3" apart. Cover with plastic wrap and let raise for 10 minutes.
5. Lightly brush tops with egg wash (1 egg plus 1 tsp water mixed).
6. Sprinkle with toppings if desired such as poppy seeds or toasted sesame seeds.
7. Bake for 10 – 12 minutes or until golden brown.
8. Buns can be frozen in an airtight container if desired. Just put them in freezer prior to raising – then take out and thaw prior to baking.

We Love Hummus

This is the perfect companion to fresh flatbread or pita bread. I always thought homemade hummus was too hard to make, but in reality, it's super easy and tastes way better than store bought.

Ingredients:
- 1 – 15 oz can chickpeas (garbanzo beans)
- ¼ cup fresh lemon juice (about 1 lemon)
- ¼ cup tahini
- ½ of a large garlic clove – minced
- 2 Tbsp olive oil, plus some for serving
- ½ to 1 tsp kosher salt
- ½ tsp ground cumin
- 2 – 3 Tbsp water
- Dash of ground paprika

Directions:
1. In the bowl of a food processor, combine tahini and lemon juice. Process for 1 minute. Scrape sides and bottom of bowl, then process for 30 seconds. Should be creamy and smooth.
2. Add the olive oil, minced garlic, cumin, and salt into the whipped tahini mixture. Process for 30 seconds, scrape sides again, and process for another 30 seconds.
3. Open can of chickpeas, drain liquid, and then rinse well with water. Add ½ of the chickpeas to the food processor, then process for 1 minute. Scrape bowl, add the rest of the chickpeas, and process for 1 – 2 minutes until thick and smooth.
4. To serve: scrape hummus into a bowl and drizzle about 1 Tbsp of olive oil over the top. Sprinkle with paprika.
5. Will keep for 1 week in the fridge if stored in an airtight container.

Awesome Baked Fish and Chips

When we featured the British Isles one month in the restaurant, Aaron worked hard to find and fine-tune a great baked fish and chips. This has awesome flavor without the frying and fat.

Ingredients:

- 2 lbs. cod, cut into serving size pieces
- 2 cups panko breadcrumbs +2 Tbsp flour (Aaron used Italian seasoned bread crumbs as he liked that flavor better)
- 1 egg
- 1 egg white
- ½ tsp garlic salt
- ½ tsp onion powder
- ⅛ tsp black pepper
- ½ tsp lemon Mrs. Dash spice mix
- Cooking spray

Directions:

1. Heat oven to 450°F.
2. Line a large cookie sheet with foil and spray with cooking spray.
3. Beat egg and egg white into a flat bowl.
4. Place panko in a flat bowl with seasonings.
5. Dip fish into egg, then into panko, pressing panko into the fish.
6. Place fish on the cookie sheet. After all the fish is coated and on the tray, spray with cooking spray.
7. Bake for approximately 15 minutes until coating is nicely browned and fish is done. It should flake easily.
8. Serve with your favorite seasoned baked potato wedges. Add a slice of lemon and some tartar sauce.

Inspired by food.com

Herbalicious Roasted Potatoes

We have used these potatoes for breakfast, as well as served them as a side dish for some of the dinner recipes. The key ingredient is lots of fresh herbs.

Ingredients
- 1 lb. potatoes (fingerlings, small white or red potatoes work best)
- 1 Tbsp fresh rosemary
- 1 Tbsp fresh chives and/or parsley
- 1 tsp Italian Seasoning Herb Mix
- 1 tsp salt (or to taste)
- ½ tsp black pepper
- 1 Tbsp garlic powder
- 3 Tbsp light olive oil or other high temperature oil
- 2 Tbsp water

Process
1. Preheat oven to 400° F.
2. Wash and cut potatoes. Cut in quarters for breakfast, and wedges for dinner sides. (if you are using russet potatoes, you need to blanch in hot water for 5 minutes and drain.)
3. Finely chop all fresh herbs. Make sure to remove any large pieces of rosemary stems.
4. Mix all herbs, fresh and dry, together in the bottom of a large zip lock bag
5. Add olive oil and water to bag along with potato pieces.
6. Seal the bag tight and mix contents thoroughly.
7. Pour bag ingredients into a foil lined 9"x13" glass baking dish.
8. Place dish in the preheated oven and bake for 30 minutes. Use a fork to test for doneness.
9. Put in a serving dish and enjoy.

Venison Goulash

I have such fond, warm memories of eating goulash in Germany and Austria. When Mom and I traveled there for Christmas a few years ago, we enjoyed our Christmas Dinner at the Goulash Museum in Vienna, Austria. The warm spicy stew/soup is perfect on a cold blustery night. Add some homemade bread to a bowl of this soup and you won't even feel the chill. You can make this with beef if you don't have access to deer meat.

Ingredients:
- 2 lbs venison meat, cut into 1 ½ inch cubes
- 4 Tbsp flour
- 3 Tbsp pork fat *You can get this from cooking 4 strips of chopped bacon.*
- 1 large onion, chopped
- 2 garlic cloves, chopped
- 2 tsp paprika
- 1 tsp smoked paprika
- 1 tsp cayenne pepper
- ½ cup mild red wine
- 4 ¼ cups vegetable broth, room temp
- ¾ cup tomato paste (1 – small can is okay)
- Salt to taste

Directions:
1. Cook 4 strips of chopped bacon until done. Remove from the grease and set aside.
2. Cook onion and garlic in the bacon grease until cooked and soft. Remove and set aside.
3. Toss meat cubes in flour and spices (we use a zip lock bag). Add meat to bacon grease in skillet and cook until browned and sticking to pan.
4. Remove meat and de-glaze pan with red wine, scraping the bottom to get the browned bits. Add broth and tomato paste. Bring to a boil.
5. Put in a crock pot, and add in meat, cooked bacon, onions and garlic. Cook on low for several hours.

Pizza Dough and Variations

When we started our weekend restaurant we wanted to add some form of pizza. We settled on a German style pizza called flammkuchen. We made our own dough, then Aaron created several unique topping combinations inspired by European classic dishes.

It all starts with the dough. This recipe is enough for 4 small pizzas:
Ingredients:
- 6 cups all-purpose flour
- 1 cup semolina flour
- 1 Tbsp salt
- 1 Tbsp yeast
- 1 Tbsp sugar
- 3 cups hot water

1. Dissolve yeast, salt, and sugar in hot water. Add flour. Knead in mixer for 10 minutes. Let rest / raise for 15 minutes at room temperature.
2. Divide the dough into 4 – 6 balls, depending on the size of pizza desired. Ours were the size of a large dinner plate and were perfect for two people or one very hungry person.
3. Roll out to approximately ¼" - ½" thick. Pile them in a stack and cover with plastic wrap until ready to use. Rub oil on the wrap to keep it from sticking.
4. Preheat oven to 500°F. Dust your pizza stone with a sprinkle of cornmeal or semolina flour. Put pizza round on a hot pizza stone or pizza pan and pre-bake for 1 ½ minutes.
5. Add toppings from one of the three flammkuchen options. Bake approximately 7 minutes and enjoy.

Caprice Variation:
1. Spread pre-baked pizza crust with 1 Tbsp tomato paste. Aaron chose tomato paste instead of pizza sauce or marinara, so the acidity balanced with the richness of

the other ingredients.
2. Add 6 slices of fresh mozzarella cheese.
3. Spread 4 sliced Kalamata olives on top.
4. Sprinkle with 1 tsp capers (drained).
5. Bake for 7 minutes at 450°F. (Vary according to quantity of toppings and thickness of crust. Cheese should be melted, and crust should be browned.)
6. Garnish with thinly sliced fresh basil, and cherry tomato halves.
7. Drizzle with olive oil and serve.

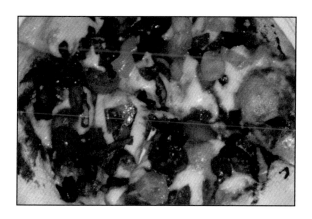

Roulade Flammkuchen Flatbread Variation:
1. Start with the meat marinade. Combine 3 cloves chopped garlic, 1 tsp pepper, 1 tsp smoked paprika, 1 Tbsp Worcestershire sauce, 2 Tbsp red wine vinegar, and 3 Tbsp olive oil.
2. Add 1 – 2 lbs. thin sliced steak chunks. Marinate for 30 minutes. (**This makes enough for 4 pizzas – adjust quantities for less pizzas**)
3. Bake or fry 2 slices of bacon (in the oven or on the stove). Bacon should be almost fully cooked but still a bit rubbery. It will finish cooking and crisp up during the pizza baking time. Chop. Set aside
4. Remove meat from marinade and drain. Then pat dry. Grill / fry marinated meat strips for 5 minutes or until done, but not overly browned. It will cook more on the pizza.
5. While the meat is cooking prepare the sauce. For this

recipe we used a fresh mustard aioli. Combine 1 Tbsp lemon juice, 3 cloves chopped garlic, 1 cup mayonnaise, 1 Tbsp olive oil, 1 Tbsp stone ground mustard.

6. Assembly for each pizza: Spread aioli on pre-baked pizza crust. Cover with ½ cup Mozzarella Cheese, ⅛ red onion sliced thin, and 2 oz of sliced meat.

7. Spread 1/4 cup of spicy bread & butter pickles (cut in ¼'s) over the top. **Do not omit the pickles**. Try it – you'll love it!

8. Bake at 450°F for 10 – 15 minutes.

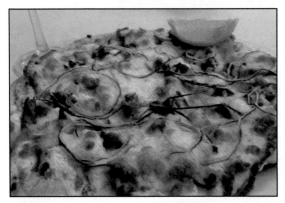

Smoked Salmon Bagels & Lox Variation:
Note: You will need some type of smoked or cured salmon for this recipe. We have provided one of Aaron's favorite options next.

1. In a small bowl, combine 4 oz cream cheese (softened), 1 Tbsp fresh chopped dill, and 1 Tbsp capers (drained and chopped).

2. Spread this mixture on your pre-baked pizza crust. This is the "sauce".

3. Top with 1 cup shredded mozzarella cheese and 2 Tbsp grated parmesan cheese. Add 2 oz smoked salmon per pizza and thinly sliced red onion (to taste), separated in rings.
4. Bake @ 500°F for 8 – 10 minutes on a preheated stone or pizza pan, sprinkled with corn meal.
5. Remove from oven, cut into slices. Squeeze juice from ½ lemon over the pizza just before serving. Mmm…mmm!!

Beet & Horseradish Cured Salmon

Ingredients:
- ¾ cup grated horseradish, well drained
- 1 salmon fillet, skin on (should be about 3 pounds)
- 1 pound red beets, raw, peeled and grated including juice
- 1 large bunch fresh dill, roughly chopped
- ½ cup + 2 tbsp sugar
- 1 cup + 2 tbsp kosher salt
- ½ tsp cracked black pepper

Directions:
1. Remove pin bones from salmon and set aside.
2. In a large stainless steel or glass bowl, combine beets, horseradish, and remaining ingredients, wearing gloves to avoid your hands turning purple.
3. In a glass 9x13 baking dish lined with plastic wrap, spread a thin layer of the beet mixture on the bottom. Lay the salmon skin side down on top. Cover the flesh with the remaining beet mixture.
4. Cover with plastic wrap, place another 9x13 on top, and weigh it down with several heavy cans. Cure in the refrigerator for 3 days.
5. When ready to use, gently scrape off beet mixture and discard.
6. You may refrigerate and serve the salmon like this or take it an extra step and smoke the salmon fillet for extra wonderful flavor.

7. Slice or flake and use on the Bagels and Lox pizza or other fine salmon dishes. Will last 1 week in refrigerator.
8. Aaron also liked to "smoke" the salmon in gin. You can Google options to see how this is done.

Inspired by Brian Polcyn

Aaron photographing the Rouladen Flammkuchen

Chicken Schnitzel with Spätzle and Fresh Basil Cream Sauce

I love schnitzel. It is one of my favorite things to eat while traveling in Germany and Austria. Each region of these countries has their own twist and variation on this century's old classic dish. For us, it came down to having a surplus of spicy potato chips left over from an event and a sale on chicken at the local market. What shall we make? This is what Aaron came up with.

Ingredients:
- Boneless, skinless chicken breasts
- 3 Tbsp butter
- ½ cup milk
- ½ cup dried Italian bread crumbs
- ½ cup jalapeno potato chips, crushed
- 3 Tbsp butter
- 1 clove garlic, minced
- ½ cup chicken broth
- ½ cup white wine
- 1 cup heavy whipping cream

- ⅓ cup grated Parmesan cheese
- ¼ cup chopped fresh basil
- ⅛ tsp black pepper
- Spätzle (boxed is okay unless you really want to make your own)

Directions:
1. Pound each chicken breast to an even ½" thickness.
2. Place milk and crushed chips in separate, shallow bowls.
3. In a large skillet, heat butter on medium heat until melted. Dip chicken in milk, then coat with crumbs. Cook chicken in butter on both sides, until cooked through (10 minutes +/-). Remove from skillet and keep warm in low oven (300°F).
4. Add the garlic to skillet and cook for 30 seconds over medium heat. Add the chicken broth and wine. Bring to a boil over medium-high heat and stir to loosen any browned bits from the bottom of the pan. Stir in cream. Boil and stir for 1 minute. Reduce heat.
5. Add Parmesan cheese, basil, and pepper. Stir sauce and cook until heated through. Remember that for a thicker sauce all you have to do is to cook it a bit longer. Aaron cooked his for about 5 minutes. Turn off the heat and let stand for a minute and it will thicken a bit more.
6. You can also cook the sauce on low in a crockpot. Put browned garlic, chicken broth, wine, cheese, spices, and cream, and keep warm until chicken and spaetzle are ready.
7. Cook spätzle according to box instructions. Drain and plate spätzle, then cooked chicken with sauce on top. Garnish with thinly sliced basil if desired. We served ours with oven roasted asparagus. Enjoy!

Inspired by Life in the Lofthouse

VEGETARIAN LOBSTER BISQUE

This very special, decadent dish was modified and prepared to be served at our first Valentines Dinner. Aaron created it as a "love offering" to his girlfriend (now wife), Lindsey.

Ingredients:
- Select 3 - 5 oz dried lobster mushrooms (or 2 cups fresh if you can find them)
- 1 quart vegetarian broth
- 2 large shallots
- 2 medium carrots
- 2 stalks celery
- 3 cloves garlic, minced
- 4 Tbsp butter
- 2 Tbsp flour
- 1 Tbsp Old Bay seasoning
- 1 cup dry white wine (chardonnay is best)
- 2 large Roma tomatoes
- 1 cup cream
- Fresh parsley for garnish
- Salt and pepper to taste

Directions:
1. If you are using dried mushrooms, reconstitute them in 3 cups of broth. Bring to a boil and simmer or 30 minutes. Save the liquid as your broth in the bisque.
2. Roughly chop the shallots, carrots, and celery.
3. Add the veggies and 3 Tbsp of butter to a large pot on medium. Cook, stirring often. You don't want them to brown - just cook. Add minced garlic and cook for 1 minute.
4. Add the remaining 1 Tbsp of butter and then flour, and Old Bay seasoning, making a roux. Cook for 1 minute.
5. Next, add wine, tomatoes, and reserved mushroom/veggie broth. Bring to a boil, then immediately reduce heat and simmer for 20 minutes.
6. Roughly chop the mushrooms – DO NOT mince. Reserve a few nice, pretty, larger pieces for the center of the soup. It should look just like a piece of lobster meat.
7. After the 20 minutes – blend the pot with an immersion blender or take out in batches and blend in a blender.
8. Finally, you get to add the lobster mushrooms and the cream. Stir. Increase heat to medium for a minute, and it's done.
9. Ladle into bowls, add the pretty lobster mushroom in the middle, and garnish with some fresh minced parsley, salt and pepper.

Although this photo has nothing to do with Bisque, it shows Rachel fixing her first Thanksgiving turkey dinner for B&B guests Ralph & Shelly.

Guinness Beef Stew with Dumplings

When Aaron was cooking in the summer patio restaurant, he selected a different region each month to feature for his special of the day. This recipe was a favorite during British Isles month. We paired it with some great dark beer.

Stew Ingredients:
- 2 lbs stew meat / beef chuck
- ¼ lb Applewood smoked bacon
- 1 onion, finely chopped
- 1 stick celery, chopped
- 2 carrots, peeled and chopped
- 2 cloves garlic, thinly sliced
- 2 turnips, peeled and diced
- 2 parsnips, diced
- 4 oz tomato paste
- 12 oz Guinness extra stout or other dark beer
- 4 cups low sodium beef broth
- 2 Tbsp Worcestershire sauce
- 1 bay leaf
- 3 sprigs thyme
- Chopped parsley
- ½ lb cremini mushrooms, sliced

Dumplings Ingredients:
- 1 ½ cups self-rising four
- ½ tsp garlic powder
- ¼ cup shortening
- ½ cup shredded sharp cheddar cheese
- 2/3 cup milk
- 3 tsp dried Italian seasonings

Directions:

1. Cook the bacon in a large, heavy-based pot over medium heat. Remove and set aside. Leave bacon fat in pot.
2. Season the beef with salt and pepper and brown in the bacon fat. Remove beef from the pot and set aside.
3. In the same pot, cook the onion, celery, and carrots until soft and fragrant, adding a little oil if necessary.
4. Add garlic and cook for another 30 seconds. Add in the tomato paste and stir.
5. Pour in the Guinness and Worcestershire sauce. Allow to come to a simmer and stir, scraping any browned bits from the pot.
6. Add the beef back to the pot and pour in the beef stock. Add the bay leaf and thyme.
7. Reduce to a simmer and cover. Simmer for 1 ½ hours. Add the carrot, parsnips, and turnips. Simmer for another 1 ½ hours, or until vegetables are tender. Remove the bay leaf and thyme branches. I believe you could also accomplish step seven in a crock pot and just leave it on low for 6 hours.
8. Add mushrooms last and cook for 10 minutes uncovered.
9. For the dumplings, stir together the self-rising flour and garlic powder in a medium bowl. Cut in the shortening until mixture resembles coarse crumbs. Stir in the cheddar cheese. Add the milk and stir until dry ingredients are moistened.
10. Make small balls with the dough and add them to the stew. Remember, they will expand/grow as they steam / cook. Cover and cook for 25 minutes on low or until dumplings are firm. You can also boil them for 10 minutes in beef broth.
11. Garnish stew with parsley and serve!

Inspired by Host The Toast

Hot German Style Pretzels
Nothing says "German cuisine" more than a hot, salty pretzel.

Ingredients:
- 2 ¾ cups all-purpose flour
- 1 tsp salt
- 1 tsp of sugar
- 1 package active dry yeast (fast-rising or regular)
- 1 cup hot tap water + 3 tbsp

Baking Soda Wash
- 2 Tbsp hot tap water and 2 tsp baking soda

Optional
- 3 Tbsp melted butter
- Course Sea salt

Directions:
1. Preheat oven to 500°F. Put all the dough ingredients in your mixer with the dough hook and knead for 5 minutes. Dough should be smooth and pliable and spring back when touched with your finger.
2. Pat into a ball and place in a lightly greased bowl. Cover with wrap and place in a warm, dark place to raise. About 40 – 60 minutes.
3. Remove dough and roll it into a thick log. Cut into 8 equal pieces and roll each piece to about 10" in length.
4. Make your baking soda wash by mixing your water and baking soda.
5. Twist your rolled dough logs into a pretzel shape. If you need help with this, Google a YouTube video. Basically, you make a horse shoe shape – bring the ends together – make two twists – bring the twists up to the top and secure.
6. Brush or dip the entire pretzel with the baking soda wash.
7. Bake for 9 minutes. They should be golden brown.
8. Remove from the oven and brush with melted butter (optional) and sprinkle with salt.
9. Serve these pretzels with course ground mustard or beer-cheese dipping sauce.

Homemade Flatbread – Greek Pita
Serve with Hummus – page 54

Ingredients: (Makes 6 - 8)
- 2 tsp instant yeast
- 1 tsp sugar
- 2/3 cup hot tap water
- ½ cup warm milk (about 100°F)
- 1 Tbsp extra-virgin olive oil
- 1 tsp salt
- 3 cups flour

Directions:

1. In your mixer bowl (with the dough hook), mix the yeast, sugar, water, milk, oil, salt, and one cup of the flour until well combined.
2. Gradually add the remaining flour until a soft dough is formed. Knead on low for 5 minutes until soft and smooth.
3. Place dough in a lightly greased bowl and cover with plastic wrap. Let it raise for 1 hour.
4. Divide dough into 6 – 8 equal pieces. Cover dough and let rest for 10 – 15 minutes.
5. Working with one piece at a time, on a lightly floured surface, roll the dough about ⅛" thick into a circle, about 7 – 8" in diameter.
6. Pre-heat a griddle or skillet to medium. Cook flatbread on hot griddle for 2 – 3 minutes on the first side until it bubbles and puffs. Use tongs to flip it over and cook on the second side until golden.
7. Transfer to a plate and cover with a clean kitchen towel.
8. Flatbread can be made, cooked, cooled, and frozen with good results.

Creamy German Salad Dressing

The creamy salad dressing found in Germany is unlike anything I've had anywhere else in the world. It is so simple, but you'll wonder how you ever existed without it after you get a taste. We love to serve this on a simple wedge salad, garnished with grated carrots, cucumbers, cherry tomato, and a few black olives. You can also add a hardboiled egg, pickled asparagus or radishes. It is so simple, but fresh, and tasty.

Ingredients:
- ¼ cup whole cream or half-n-half
- 2 tsp fresh lemon juice
- 2 tsp sugar
- Salt and pepper, to taste

Directions:
1. Whisk the first three ingredients together until the sugar dissolves. Add a little milk if necessary to thin.
2. Pour on salad immediately prior to serving.
3. This dressing is best on crisp lettuce types such as Iceberg or Romaine. Leaf lettuce does not hold up and gets soggy with this dressing.

4 DESSERT

Desserts play a huge part in any special occasion in life. Whether it's your first birthday cake, a hand-crafted wedding cake, or a holiday Yule log, ending a special event with something sweet just puts "the icing on the cake," so to speak. Raising our kids, desserts often connected us to our mothers and grandmothers as sweet family favorites. Pecan pie and oatmeal cake were recipes passed down through generations, shaped by our individual history and culture.

When we travel in Europe, dessert is always part of the daily routine, typically eaten during an afternoon coffee and cake break sitting in a sidewalk cafe. It could be an apple strudel, pudding, or my all-time favorite, Black Forest Cherry Cake.

Over the years, I have enjoyed sharing my love of baking in various forms of desserts. When we had the restaurant operating, Aaron and I worked hard to implement some lovely desserts that used local ingredients and tapped into our love of mixing old classics with a new modern twist.

I think though, that the true emotion that connects us to dessert is family and friends. When we are sharing a moment, and enjoying great food, we are making special memories that last a lifetime and beyond.

Fresh Peach Ice Cream

When you live in the Columbia River Gorge, it's always fun to create great food using all the wonderful fresh farm produce that is in such great abundance. This recipe uses my favorite summer fruit – sweet, tree-ripened peaches.

- 5 – 6 fresh peaches, peeled and sliced
- 1 ½ cups granulated sugar
- Juice of 1 large lemon
- 1 – 2 tsp vanilla extract
- ⅛ tsp almond extract
- 2 cups heavy cream

1. In a large bowl, mix together the peaches, sugar, lemon juice, and extracts. Let sit for about 15 minutes, stirring occasionally until the sugar is dissolved and peaches have released their juices.
2. Mash with a potato masher. Measure out 2 cups of the mashed peaches. Reserve the remaining peaches in a small bowl and chill until very cold.
3. Puree the 2 cups in a blender or food processor. Add the heavy cream and pour into a clean bowl. Cover with plastic wrap and chill until very cold.
4. Add to ice cream maker and churn according to manufacturer directions. Mix in the reserved peaches 5 minutes before it is done. You should be able to hear it getting thicker.
5. Transfer to a container and put in the freezer for a few hours to harden before serving.
6. Makes about 1 ½ quarts.

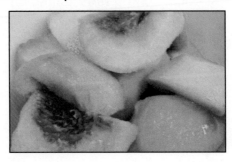

Maple Bacon Cupcakes

We love these cupcakes and have served them for several special events. Fantastic idea for Dad on Father's Day!

Ingredients:
- 1 cup flour
- 1 cup cake flour
- 1 – 4 oz box vanilla instant pudding mix
- 1 tsp baking powder
- 1 Tbsp potato starch
- 1 tsp cinnamon
- 1 tsp nutmeg
- ½ tsp salt
- ½ cup unsalted butter (room temp)
- ¾ cup light brown sugar – packed
- ¾ cup sugar
- 1 ½ tsp vanilla extract
- 4 large egg whites (room temp)
- ¼ cup real maple syrup
- ½ cup half-n-half (room temp)
- ½ cup bacon, cooked and chopped

Frosting:
- 1 – 8 oz cream cheese (room temp)
- 2 Tbsp unsalted butter (room temp)
- 2 cups powdered sugar
- ¼ cup real maple syrup
- 2 tsp ground cinnamon
- 3 slices bacon, cooked and chopped

Directions:
1. Preheat oven to 325°F.
2. Place paper liners in a 12-cup muffin tin.
3. To prepare the cupcakes, combine flours, pudding mix, baking powder, potato starch, cinnamon, nutmeg and salt in a bowl with a whisk.
4. In a separate bowl, cream the butter and sugars with a

mixer on low speed until combined – 6 to 8 minutes. Gradually mix in the vanilla and egg whites. Scrape down the sides of the bowl; continue mixing until light and fluffy.

5. Add the flour mixture in 3 batches, alternating with the maple syrup and half-n-half, mixing after each addition and ending with flour. Mix until ingredients are combined – but not overmixed.

6. Fold in the bacon. Pour the batter into the prepared muffin tin, filling each cup about ¾ full. Bake until a toothpick comes out clean. About 15 – 20 minutes, depending on your oven.

7. Cool completely.

8. Meanwhile, make the frosting by beating the cream cheese and butter with a mixer on medium speed until creamy.

9. Add the powdered sugar, maple syrup, and cinnamon; beat until combined.

10. After the cupcakes are cooled, spread or pipe on the frosting and top with chopped bacon.

Inspired by food.com

Carrot Cake Cupcakes with
Brown Sugar Cream Cheese Frosting

This makes a great Easter cupcake. Carrots, rabbits, Easter!

Ingredients:
- 1 cup flour
- 1 tsp baking soda
- 1 ½ tsp cinnamon
- ¼ tsp salt
- ⅓ cup vegetable oil
- ¼ cup unsweetened applesauce
- ¼ cup brown sugar
- ½ cup sugar
- 2 large eggs
- 1 tsp vanilla extract
- 1 ½ cups finely grated carrots (about 2 med carrots)

Frosting:
- 8 oz cream cheese
- 4 Tbsp unsalted butter
- ¾ cup brown sugar
- ½ cup powdered sugar
- ½ tsp vanilla extract

Directions:
1. For cupcakes, preheat oven to 350° F. Line a 12-count muffin tin with paper liners. Set aside.
2. Combine flour, baking soda, cinnamon, and salt. Set aside.
3. In a large bowl, beat oil, applesauce, brown sugar, granulated sugar, eggs, and vanilla until thoroughly combined. Add dry ingredients and beat until combined. Stir in carrots.
4. Divide batter evenly among muffin cups. Bake for 18-20 minutes, until a toothpick comes out clean. Cool for 10 minutes, then remove to cool completely on a wire rack.
5. For frosting, place all frosting ingredients in a large bowl. Beat with an electric mixer on low speed, then

gradually increase speed to med-high. Beat for two minutes, until smooth and creamy. If you prefer it thicker, just add more powdered sugar.
6. Spread or pipe the frosting on the top of each cupcake.
7. Store in the fridge and bring to room temp before serving.

Raspberry Swirled Cheesecake Mini Cupcakes

I love to make this in my mini cupcake pan and use them with the Sugar Cookie Lemon Tarts on page 81. You could adapt this to larger cupcakes or make a full-size tart by adjusting the cooking time.

Ingredients:
Crust
- ¾ cup+ 2 Tbsp graham cracker crumbs
- 1 ½ tsp granulated sugar
- 3 ½ Tbsp salted butter, melted

Raspberry Swirl
- 4 oz fresh raspberries
- 2 Tbsp granulated sugar

Cheesecake filling
- ¾ cup granulated sugar
- 1 Tbsp all-purpose flour
- 2 (8 oz) pkgs cream cheese, softened
- 1 tsp lemon zest
- 2 large eggs
- 1 tsp vanilla extract
- ¼ cup sour cream

Directions:
1. Preheat oven to 325° F.
2. To make the crust, use a fork to stir together the graham cracker crumbs, and sugar. Then pour in the melted butter until evenly moistened. Add 1 slightly heaping tablespoonful to paper lined muffin cups. Press crust firmly into an even layer. Bake in preheated oven for 5 minutes. Remove and cool.
3. For the raspberry swirl, put raspberries and sugar in food processor and pulse until well pureed, about 30 seconds. Press mixture through a fine mesh strainer into a bowl to remove seeds. Set aside.
4. For the cheesecake filling, whisk tougher granulated

sugar and flour. Add cream cheese and lemon zest and blend until smooth. Mix in eggs one at a time. Stir in vanilla and sour cream until combined. Tap bowl forcefully against countertop about 10 times to release air bubbles.

5. Divide mixture evenly among cups over the crust layer. Jiggle pan to level cheesecake, then dollop about 3 – 5 drops of raspberry sauce over each cupcake (about ¾ tsp). Using a toothpick, swirl raspberry filling with cheesecake mixture to create a marbled design.

6. Bake in preheated oven 22 – 25 minutes until cupcakes are puffed and nearly set (they might crack a little). Remember to adjust baking time if using mini cupcake tin or large full-size cake tin. In my regular oven it took 16 minutes. In a convection oven it takes about 18 minutes.

7. Remove from oven and allow to cool. Then chill in the refrigerator for 3 hours to set.

Inspired by www.cookingclassy.com (from Annie's Eats)

Sugar Cookie Lemon Tarts

This is a great little tart for a brunch, lunch, or afternoon treat.

Crust
- Tbsp unsalted butter, softened
- ½ cup granulated sugar
- 1 egg
- 1 ½ cup all-purpose flour
- ¼ tsp baking powder
- Pinch salt

Lemon filling
- 2 eggs
- 3 egg yolks
- ¼ cup heavy whipping cream
- Juice from 1 large lemon
- ¼ cup granulated sugar

Topping
- 4 Tbsp powdered sugar, divided
- ½ cup heavy whipping cream
- OR – use a can of purchased whip cream if you are transporting these to a potluck or special event

Directions:
1. For crust, beat butter and sugar in a mixer until light and fluffy. Add the egg and mix until fully incorporated. Add the flour, baking powder, and salt all at once and mix on medium until no spots of flour remain. Do not overmix. Wrap the dough in plastic wrap and refrigerate for 30 minutes.
2. Preheat the oven to 350°F. Lightly grease a mini muffin tin with cooking spray.
3. To make the filling, whisk together the eggs, egg yolks, whipping cream, lemon juice, and sugar until smooth.
4. Remove dough from the fridge. Divide into quarters and divide each quarter into six even balls of dough. Press each ball into the space in the muffin tin. Using your

thumbs, press the dough until it is evenly distributed along the sides and bottom (making a little cup). Pour lemon filling into the center of each sugar cookie cup, stopping just below the top.

5. Bake until the filling is set, and the crust begins to turn golden, 10 – 12 minutes. Do not overbake. Watch them carefully and pull them out when you start to see the crusts turning brown. Allow to cool at room temperature. Refrigerate until ready to serve.

6. Before serving, dust the tops of tarts with powdered sugar.

7. To make fresh whip cream, beat the whipping cream with the remaining 2 Tbsp of sugar until stiff peaks form. Pipe or spoon whipped cream on top of each tart. Serve chilled.

Inspired by Inquiring Chef

Aaron and Rachel
2014

Gluten-free Rhubarb Bars

Ingredients
- 2 cups gluten-free flour (Bob's Red Mill 1 to 1 Baking Flour)
- tsp baking powder
- ½ cup cold butter
- 2 eggs, beaten
- 3 Tbsp milk
- 5 cups sliced fresh or frozen rhubarb (thaw if frozen)
- 1 – 3oz package strawberry gelatin

Topping:
- 1 cup sugar
- 1 cup gluten-free Bob's Red Mill 1-to-1 Baking flour
- ½ cup cold unsalted butter

Directions:
1. Preheat oven to 375°F.
2. In a bowl, combine flour and baking powder. Cut in butter until mixture resembles coarse crumbs.
3. Stir in eggs and milk until moistened. Press into the bottom of a 9 x 13, sprayed with cooking spray.
4. Top with rhubarb then sprinkle with gelatin.
5. For topping, combine sugar and flour. Cut in butter until coarse crumbs form. Sprinkle over the top.
6. Bake at 375°F for 35 – 40 minutes or until lightly browned.
7. Cool on wire rack. Cut into bars. Makes 2-3 dozen depending on what size you want.

Slow Cooker Wedding Hot Cocoa

This is a big hit as the final evening beverage after a cool outdoor wedding or special event. Having it ready to go in the crock pot makes it super simple. This makes a great holiday drink.

Aaron and Lindsey made this for Lindsey's family for Christmas one year and ended up running to the store for more ingredients to make a second batch because everyone loved it so much.

This recipe makes about 12 servings. I like to serve this with fresh whipped cream, peppermint chunks, marshmallows, and sprinkles. Each person can then add their own toppings to taste.

Ingredients:
- 2/3 cup of hot water
- ½ cup of cocoa – Hershey's natural unsweetened
- 1 - 14 oz can sweetened condensed milk
- ½ cup of heavy cream
- 6 cups of whole milk
- ½ cup of sugar
- 2 tsp vanilla extract
- Dash of salt

Directions:
1. In a small bowl, combine hot water and cocoa. Stir until smooth.
2. Combine all ingredients in your slow cooker, including the cocoa mixture. Whisk to combine.
3. Heat on low for about 3 hours, stirring occasionally.
4. Serve with your favorite toppings and enjoy!

Inspired by www.number-2-pencil.com

Vanilla Bean Ice Cream

This ice cream became a staple in the restaurant. It was great served on fresh peach cobbler or spicy apple crisp. What makes the flavor unique is the cream cheese. Aaron searched hard for this recipe because his Dad, David, doesn't like custard – egg yolk based ice cream.

Ingredients:
- 2 cups whole milk
- 1 Tbsp + 1 tsp cornstarch
- 1 ½ oz cream cheese (softened – 3 Tbsp)
- 1 ¼ cups heavy cream
- 2/3 cup sugar
- 1 ½ Tbsp light corn syrup
- 1 vanilla bean, split and seeds scraped
- ⅛ tsp kosher salt

Directions:
1. Fill a large bowl with ice water.
2. In a small bowl, mix 2 Tbsp of the milk with the cornstarch.
3. In a separate large bowl, whisk the cream cheese until smooth.
4. In a large saucepan, combine the remaining milk with the heavy cream, sugar, corn syrup, and vanilla bean and seeds. Bring the milk mixture to a boil and cook over moderate heat until the sugar dissolves and the vanilla flavors the milk, about 4 minutes.
5. Take off the heat, gradually whisk in the cornstarch mixture. Return to a boil and cook over med-high heat until the mixture is slightly thickened, about 1 minute.
6. Gradually whisk the hot milk mixture into the cream cheese until smooth. Whisk in the salt. Set the bowl in the ice water bath and let stand, stirring occasionally, until cold, about 20 minutes.
7. Strain the ice cream base into an ice cream maker and freeze according to manufacturer's instructions.
8. Pack ice cream in freezer container until ready to serve.

Saffron Pistachio Ice Cream

Aaron loves his collection of spices and was particularly excited about this ice cream, which showcased his favorite spice. It was a customer favorite. He used the vanilla bean ice cream on page 85 as the base for this unique flavor option.

Grind together 1 tsp sugar and a pinch of saffron threads in a mortar. Grind until saffron breaks down.

Add sugar and saffron mixture to the cream mixture in Step 4. Mix to combine.

Continue steps as listed on page 85.

After it cools, strain to remove left over saffron threads – if any.

During the last 2 minutes of churning, add ½ cup of shelled, and chopped pistachios.

Remove from the ice cream maker (it will be soft) and put in the freezer for 2 hours until ready to serve.

Chocolate Raspberry Coconut Almond Tart
(Gluten-Free and Vegan)

One of the things I love the most about owning and operating a B&B, is getting the opportunity to do special things for special people. This recipe came from a very unique dinner that I created and prepared for a couple celebrating their 50th wedding anniversary. They had some very strict dietary needs, so with Aaron's help, I developed a full course dinner menu just for them. This was served in our historic, brick Ice House (circa 1881), complete with music and candles.

This can be made in mini-tarts or full-size by adjusting the baking time.

Ingredients:
Crust
- ½ cup unsweetened coconut flakes
- ¼ cup almond meal/flour
- ¼ cup coconut flour
- ¼ tsp salt
- 2 Tbsp coconut oil
- 2 Tbsp agave syrup

Filling
- 1 cup canned coconut milk
- 8 oz bittersweet chocolate, finely chopped
- 4 oz semi-sweet chocolate
- 1 tsp vanilla extract

Topping
- 1 cup fresh raspberries
- Whipped coconut milk (or canned whip cream)

Directions:
1. Preheat oven to 350°F.
2. To make the crust, use a food processor to combine coconut flakes, almond meal and salt. Pulse to combine.

3. In a small container, melt the coconut oil and agave syrup together. Pour into the food processor and pulse until well mixed.
4. Press the crust into the bottom and sides of either a 9" tart pan or individual tart pans. Use the flat bottom of a cup to press hard.
5. Bake crust for 10 – 12 minutes (large tart pan) and 7 – 8 minutes (smaller tart pans).
6. For the filling, place the chopped chocolate in a medium mixing bowl. Set aside.
7. In a saucepan, bring the coconut milk to boil gently. Pour the milk over the chopped chocolate and let stand for 2 minutes before stirring until smooth and creamy. Stir in the vanilla extract.
8. Pour the chocolate ganache into the cooled tart shell. Chill until set, at least 2 hours.
9. Top with fresh raspberries and whip cream rosettes. Serve.

Inspired by Blahnik Baker

Connie's Famous Schwarzwälder Kirschtorte
(Black Forest Cherry Cake)

This recipe was inspired by the many times we stopped to enjoy an afternoon cake and coffee break in a quaint little German town. It soon became our most popular dinner dessert at the restaurant. It has everything a cake should have; great taste and a simple, elegant presentation with that wow factor that will have your guests asking, "Did you make this?"

Cake Ingredients:
- 2 cups all-purpose flour
- 2 cups sugar
- ¾ cup unsweetened cocoa powder
- 2 tsp baking powder
- ½ tsp baking soda
- 1 tsp salt
- 1 tsp finely ground coffee beans
- 1 cup half-n-half
- ½ cup vegetable oil
- 2 eggs
- 2 tsp vanilla extract
- 1 cup boiling water

Cake directions:
1. Preheat your oven to 350° F. Prepare three 8" cake pans by spraying with baking spray or lining with paper cake liners. (Note: I always make this in three pans to

89

get 3 layers in my finished cakes).

2. Combine flour, sugar, cocoa, baking powder, baking soda, salt, and coffee in a large stand mixer bowl. Stir to combine well.
3. Add milk, vegetable oil, eggs, and vanilla to flour mixture and mix on medium speed until well combined.
4. Reduce speed and carefully add boiling water to the cake batter. Beat on high for 1 minute to add air to the batter. (I draped a dish towel over my mixer during this process, so it didn't spatter chocolate cake batter all over myself and the kitchen.)
5. Distribute cake batter evenly between the three prepared cake pans. Tap gently on the counter to get out any large air bubbles.
6. Bake for 30 – 35 minutes, until a toothpick comes out clean when inserted in the center.
7. Remove and cool for 10 minutes. Then remove from pans and cool completely on a wire rack.

For the full cake you will now need 2 cans of dark sweet pitted cherries. This is not cherry pie filling – but canned cherries in heavy syrup. You will also need some Kirschwasser, which is an alcohol-based cherry flavored brandy. How much depends on how strong you want this flavor to be. In Germany there are actually laws about the percentage of alcohol in this cake. If you want to leave out the brandy, it will still work, but it will be lacking the true Schwarzwälder Kirschtorte flavor.

Drain the cherry juice from the can into a small saucepan. Add 3 Tbsp of cherry brandy. Heat on medium – high to reduce until syrupy and thick.

In your stand mixer with a wire whip attachment, add 1 pint of heavy whipping cream and ¼ cup of powdered sugar. Whip on high until peaks form and the whip cream is smooth and stiff.

Now, let's put this all together.
1. Level and/or torte your cake layers. I use 3 layers.
2. Put down one layer on a cardboard cake round or on your cake serving platter.
3. Drain any remaining liquid from canned cherries. Carefully line up cherries from one can over the entire layer. Stop ½" from the edge so the cherries don't spill out when you add the next layer. Now drizzle the cherries and cake with some of the reduced cherry juice/brandy mixture. I use about ¼ cup over the whole layer. Don't apply it too close to the edge or it will get soggy and collapse. You just want to give some of that rich flavor and add some moisture to the cake layers.
4. Add your next layer and repeat the process.
5. Now, add your top layer.
6. Using your large frosting spatula, start to apply the whipped cream to the sides of the cake. It should be smooth and heavy. Be careful not to get cherry juice on the whip cream or it turns pink. Finish off by adding whip cream to the top. Smooth out or add little "waves" to the whip cream to create a pattern. I have also piped rosettes on the top and sides. It is really up to you.
7. Chill. The cake is now ready to cut and serve. It will last in the refrigerator for several days providing you keep it in an air tight container and providing your family doesn't eat it all at once.

Crawford Family Raspberry Lemon Cheesecake

This is a recipe passed down through my daughter-in-law Lindsey's mother's family – The Crawford's. The women in her family love to make this cheesecake for special occasions: birthdays, anniversaries, and even Christmas! Lindsey's Aunt Nancy, Aunt Rae, and mom, Cindy, all taught her how to make this special dessert. She's since shared it with our family, and we used it for the Valentine's Day dinner for our B&B guests last year. It is so special to me that they are allowing this family legacy recipe to be included in my cookbook.

Crust:
- 1 ½ cups crushed graham crackers
- ¼ cup sugar
- ¼ cup melted butter
- ¼ tsp cinnamon

Combine and press into a 9" spring form pan. Bake at 300°F for 10 minutes.

Cheesecake Layer:
- 3 – 8 oz cream cheese, softened. Beat until creamy. Use only good quality cream cheese, the cheap ones will separate.
- 1 ½ cup sugar – gradually add into the cream cheese.
- 4 eggs
- 4 tsp vanilla
- 2 lemons – grated peel
- 5 tsp lemon juice

Combine all and mix until smooth. Bake 1 hour and 15 minutes or until firm at 300°F. Cool for 10 minutes.

Cream Layer:
- 1 ½ cups sour cream
- ⅓ cup sugar
- 1 tsp vanilla

Combine and spread over cooled cake. Bake for 5 minutes more at 300°F. Cool to room temperature, and then refrigerate at least 5 hours.

Fruit Glaze Layer:
- 10 oz frozen or fresh raspberries (thaw if frozen)
- 1 Tbsp corn starch
- ½ tsp vanilla
- ¼ tsp salt
- ¼ cup sugar
- 1 tsp lemon juice

Combine glaze ingredients. Cook until thick. Cool to room temperature with wax paper on top to prevent a film from forming. Pour onto cake and cover with wax paper again until ready to serve.

Lindsey (right) and her mom Cindy.

Aaron and Lindsey's White Wedding Cake
With Vanilla Buttercream

When Aaron proposed to his love, Lindsey, and they set their wedding date, I knew I wanted to be able to make the cake for their special day. I took some cake decorating classes and made a dozen practice cakes until I got it just right. The cake turned out beautiful and it was such an honor to share this with them on their wedding day. I have included not only the cake recipe, but the fantastic butter cream that covered it. This cake is an angel food consistency and not overly sweet.

Ingredients:
- 2 ¾ cups cake flour
- 1 ¾ cups granulated sugar
- 1 ¼ tsp baking soda
- 1 ¼ tsp baking powder
- 1 tsp salt
- 4 egg whites
- 1 ½ cups whole milk
- 1 cup sour cream
- 1 Tbsp white distilled vinegar
- 2 tsp vanilla extract

Directions:
1. Preheat the oven to 350° F. (325° for convection oven)
2. Spray 3 – 8" pans with non-stick spray
3. In a large mixing bowl, combine the flour, sugar, baking soda, baking powder, and salt.
4. In a separate bowl, whip the egg whites with an electric mixer until soft peaks form. Whip for another minute or two until the whites are not quite stiff but stay on the beaters when you lift them up. They should be quite wet, not dry.
5. Add the milk, sour cream, vinegar, and vanilla to the dry ingredients and whisk vigorously for about two minutes until well combined. Gently fold in the whipped egg whites in three additions for a light and airy batter.
6. Divide the batter between the cake pans. Mine was

three layers. Bake for about 18 – 22 minutes, until risen and toothpick comes out clean. Set the pans on wire racks, cover loosely with kitchen towel and cool for 10 minutes.

7. Remove from pans and cool completely before frosting with the buttercream. You can make these the day before and store in the refrigerator until ready to assemble on the special day.

Connie's Note: From experience, this cake held up to 80+ degree temperature at an outdoor venue! Who would have guessed it would be so hot on a May evening in Washington?

Inspired by Curly Girl Kitchen

Vanilla Wedding Buttercream

This is the perfect buttercream for decorating a special cake. I have used this for cakes and cupcakes. It will save at room temperature in an air-tight container for up to 3 days. In the fridge for up to 4 weeks. I made this buttercream every week for my cake decorating class and it never caused me any trouble in any of the applications we learned.

Ingredients:
- 1 ½ cups unsalted butter (room temp – soft)
- 1 ½ cups Crisco (or other quality solid shortening)
- 6 cups confectioners powdered sugar (almost a full bag)
- 6 Tbsp heavy cream
- 2 tsp vanilla extract
- ¼ tsp salt

Directions:
1. Combine butter and Crisco in a stand mixer with the paddle attachment.
2. Whip on medium - high for 3 minutes
3. Scrape the sides and bottom of the bowl to make sure it is evenly mixed and then add the salt. Mix well.
4. Stop mixer and add the powdered sugar all at once.
5. Mix on low speed until incorporated, scrape the bottom again and then mix on high for 3 minutes.
6. Scrape the bowl again and then while mixing on low speed, slowly drizzle in the heavy cream.
7. Increase speed to high and whip for another 5 minutes.
8. Depending on your mixer, you may need to use a batter shield to keep it from spattering out onto your walls and you ☺
9. Add the vanilla and then you are done!

Inspired by Gretchen's Bakery

EPILOGUE

Food is essential to our day-to-day life. What and how we prepare and consume that food is totally up to us. It's our attitude about what we put in our mouth that dictates our health. Even the simplest of breakfasts, if prepared with fresh, colorful ingredients, can change our whole outlook on the day. That's what I try to do with the breakfasts I prepare each morning for our guests. I want to put something on the table that makes them feel special, something that stays in their mind and heart long after they have left our B&B. And while producing this cookbook has been a little bit like making polenta; a marathon labor of love, I sincerely hope and pray that you will take these recipes and make them your own. Make it fresh. Make it colorful, and homemade, and don't forget to add the best ingredient of all…joy!

INDEX

ABOUT THE AUTHOR

Connie Nice is a wife, mother, and grandmother who delights in sharing her love of cooking, travel, family, and faith in her Connie's Corner blog. She retired from her career job to focus on her writing, and now has other published books as well as significant pieces in various online anthologies. She created this cookbook after receiving multiple requests from guests staying at the Husum Riverside Bed & Breakfast, which has been owned and operated by her family since 2015. She is currently working on a novel which she hopes to have completed soon.

www.connienice.com

Made in the USA
Lexington, KY
13 September 2018